# Corporate to Classroom

## A Career-Switcher's Guide to Teaching

FELECIA L. CHRISTIAN

ROWMAN & LITTLEFIELD EDUCATION

A Division of
ROWMAN & LITTLEFIELD PUBLISHERS, INC.
Lanham • New York • Toronto • Plymouth, UK

Published by Rowman & Littlefield Education
A division of Rowman & Littlefield Publishers, Inc.
A wholly owned subsidiary of The Rowman & Littlefield Publishing Group, Inc.
4501 Forbes Boulevard, Suite 200, Lanham, Maryland 20706
www.rowman.com

Estover Road, Plymouth PL6 7PY, United Kingdom

British Library Cataloguing in Publication Information Available

**Library of Congress Cataloging-in-Publication Data**

Christian, Felecia L.
    Corporate to classroom : a career-switcher's guide to teaching / Felecia L. Christian.
        p. cm.
    Includes bibliographical references.
    ISBN 978-1-60709-690-0 (pbk.) — ISBN 978-1-60709-691-7 (electronic)
    1. First year teachers—United States. 2. Teaching—Vocational guidance—United States. 3. Career changes—United States. I. Title.
    LB2844.1.N4C496 2012
    371.1—dc23

                                                    2011049331

♾️™ The paper used in this publication meets the minimum requirements of American National Standard for Information Sciences—Permanence of Paper for Printed Library Materials, ANSI/NISO Z39.48-1992.

Printed in the United States of America

# Contents

# Acknowledgments

I want to thank my gracious and loving God for giving me the idea to write this book and the grace to endure the extreme amounts of pressure.

Chris, I thank you for taking up the slack and loving me through writing this book and going to school. You are an awesome husband and father. I love you.

Noah and Emmanuel, there is greatness inside both of you. You are very special and handsome! Remember to always dream big and pursue your dreams.

Davonya, thank you for blazing the path.

Thank you Marcus Miller of 3DI Digital Design Group for the wonderful cover. You are amazing!

To the staff at Summer Hill and Lewis and Clark Elementary Schools, thank you for the experience. The experience has been enlightening and invaluable. You are a great group of educators.

My special thanks go to those who proofed and ripped apart the content of this book. You know who you are. You helped me give career switchers a glimpse of our world. You were brutal, and I thank you for it!

To Tom Koerner and Rowman & Littlefield Education, thanks for giving me this opportunity! Your patience and insight has been wonderful.

# Introduction

*On the Front Lines:*

I didn't know the physical, mental, and emotional impact that my first year of teaching would have. It is something you can't really prepare for. I was overwhelmed and by the spring, I was burned out.

This actually happened the first four years of my teaching career. People who have never taught think it's an easy job and that teachers don't need to have summer, winter, and spring breaks. I challenge them to walk a mile in my (or any teacher's) shoes, and then complain about our breaks.

Throughout my first year I questioned if I had made the right career choice, but I hung in there because I felt that things would improve as my experience grew. Each year I learn something new and ways to make it a better year. I love children and I love art. That's why I am still teaching.

Underwood

It is this type of sentiment about teaching that led me to write this book. There are professionals who decide to leave the corporate structure to follow their dream to teach impressionable students. They leave the corporate environment without a true understanding of what they are about to experience.

Teaching is demanding, difficult, and taxing on you mentally and emotionally. There is so much to learn and do. This is not a career choice that you should make unless you are clear on the expectations and the challenges that you may face.

For me personally, the transition from corporate to classroom was a hard one. I was not prepared for the politics, the lack of supplies, lack of training, and lack of respect that is so prevalent in many school districts. I like order and a sense of knowing what to do. I felt like many situations were chaotic and could have been handled more professionally. A concrete set of procedures and proper training could have eliminated many of these situations.

Many teachers that I encountered were burned out by lack of concern from parents, coworkers, and administration. The disapproving words and prejudgments of students, parents, and staff were appalling and heartbreaking.

I found that many teachers are disrespectful, unprofessional, and rude in meetings. This baffled me. Educators demand and expect their students to give them their undivided attention but they do not give it to others.

In one of my very first staff meetings, a teacher said, "They say teachers are the worst students." Most of the meetings, professional developments, and training sessions exemplified why the speaker had voiced that observation.

Amazingly, there are many teachers who talk about the challenges of teaching, but those same teachers express their love for it. You must love what you do to stay in education for the long haul. If you do not, you will quickly be overwhelmed and feel burned out by the amount of work that must be accomplished, while trying to remain sensitive to the needs of the students that you teach.

Most teachers will quickly tell you how difficult it is to manage a classroom, and many of them will also tell you that they could not imagine doing anything else. Even with all of its challenges, the reward far outweighs the difficult moments. This book will challenge you to prepare yourself, do your research, trigger questions that you should ask, prompt you to examine your reasons for switching careers, and help you begin your journey.

This book has some additional features—"Sticky Notes" and "On the Front Lines" segments—and the appendices are filled with useful sample forms to give you more information and tools from those who are working in the field.

*Sticky Notes:* The purpose of a sticky note is to highlight important information from the text. This invaluable information is something that you should take "note" of.

*On the Front Lines:* This feature highlights experiences from teachers, principals, and businessmen and businesswomen.

# 1

# In the Beginning

Congratulations on your decision to become an educator. This book is designed to help you really think about whether teaching is the right decision for you. There is nothing easy about educating our future.

You will be faced with challenges before the first student ever sets foot into your classroom. Being informed about the challenges and rewards will be beneficial to you and the students that you teach. It takes a special person to leave what they know, to spend time with impressionable students.

First and foremost, this profession is about the students you teach. These students will come from different backgrounds, cultures, and mindsets. You must be prepared to confront this challenge head on. You should determine what your students already know, taking into account their background or prior knowledge and culture, and connect with them at that point, so that you can take them forward.

If students are not a priority for you, then please consider staying in your corporate environment. You should not decide to teach because you need more time with family or because of the time off that you will receive throughout the year. This is a decision that must be taken seriously.

You are literally putting yourself in a position to impart wisdom to generations of young people. Their experience in your classroom can be positive or negative. It will be an experience that can influence their behaviors and decisions for years to come. Debbie Miller, the author of *Teaching with Intention*, states, "I believe we cannot underestimate the power of our

*Sticky Note: The students' experience in your classroom can influence their behaviors and decisions for years to come.*

influence—what we choose to say and do in the classroom profoundly affects the ways children view their teacher, themselves, and each other."

## ROUTES TO THE CLASSROOM

There are several routes you can take to enter the field of education. Consider what you want to teach and then evaluate the route for that particular field carefully. You must be committed to becoming a great educator. You must learn curriculums, instructional strategies, classroom management, and the standards of learning for your state. To become an educator, you

*Sticky Note: Student teaching normally requires you to be in a classroom for a full semester.*

will be required to complete an educational program and hours in a classroom as a student teacher.

To get a grasp of all that this career switch entails, visit a local college that offers an educational program. An advisor should be able to break down the course requirements, as well as the number of student teaching hours that are necessary to complete the program and obtain licensure. These requirements vary from state to state.

When doing your research you may want to discuss with your current employer whether your student teaching can be fulfilled while you are still working in your corporate position. This could be a very important aspect because most corporate positions require you to be present during the same hours that you will need to complete this portion of your educational program.

Student teaching normally requires you to be in a classroom for a full semester. During this portion of your education, you may have to find a job with evening hours or not work at all. Depending on your financial situation this may not be a feasible option for you.

## PROVISIONAL OR CONDITIONAL LICENSING

Most state education departments offer some type of career switcher program and work closely with local universities providing educational programs. Furthermore, they may offer a temporary license for those who would like to teach. One such license is a conditional or provisional license. A conditional or provisional license will allow you to teach while obtaining licensure and completing an educational program. This type of license may require as little as one class after you have completed a bachelor's degree program.

If you choose the conditional or provisional route, develop a plan for completing your educational program. When developing a timeline or plan consider the difficulty of the classes and the time-sensitive state or national exams that must be passed. Give yourself time to repeat a class or an exam.

In addition to fulfilling the educational requirements, remember, you will be teaching students in a classroom. This will require you to not only complete your school work for your education, but effectively teach a curriculum that requires lesson plans and time.

When you are planning how you will complete the educational program, be aware that some classes and exams may only be offered certain times of the year. Normally, conditional or provisional licensure is given to the licensee with a time limit attached to it. If you

*Sticky Note: A conditional or provisional license will allow you to teach while obtaining licensure and completing an educational program.*

*Sticky Note: When you are planning how you will complete the educational program, be aware that some classes and exams may only be offered certain times of the year.*

miss or fail a course and do not have time to complete the course before your time limit is up, you can put your job in jeopardy.

The conditional or provisional licensure route may be the quickest, but may also cause you the most frustration. The standards for students are high; students cannot afford to waste a year of learning while you learn what you need to know to teach them. You should go into this endeavor as prepared as possible.

If at all possible complete your education before you ever step foot into a classroom. You will find that although there will be challenges, there will be less of a learning curve with your educational process behind you. Note that your education does not prepare you for everything but it can provide strategies that will be useful in the different aspects of teaching.

## STUDENT TEACHING

The student teaching portion of the educational program is necessary to getting insight on what you may encounter in the classroom. Student teaching will give you a glimpse of the challenges that an educator encounters on a daily basis. There have been many people who have decided that teaching was not the right course of action for them because of what they experienced during their semester of student teaching.

Student teaching also gives you an opportunity to experience different grade levels, which can be instrumental in finding the level that is the best fit for your style of teaching. During this process, you should have an opportunity to create, demonstrate, and evaluate what you have learned. Take advantage of this time to find out what strategies work well for you.

## REQUIRED TEACHER ASSESSMENTS

In addition to the educational requirements, you may be required to take state or national exams. These exams normally have a fee associated with them, and the fees can vary from exam to exam. Most of these exams are offered throughout the year but may only be administered on certain dates. It can become very costly and impact your timeline if you are unable to pass these exams after a few attempts.

This is another area where you should have a plan in place. There have been teachers forced back into the corporate environment because they are unable to pass one of these exams. The inability to pass can prevent you from obtaining your license, and if you are working under a conditional license, it can cost you your job.

There are many resources available to help you study for these national and state exams. Ask the teachers who are newly licensed what they used to prepare for the exams as well. Many may still have the resources available for you to borrow.

*On the Front Lines:*

There were four tests required to complete my licensure. I heard many horror stories about people repeating a test three or more times. I was determined to pass every test the first time. I went to the testing proctor's website and pulled all of the sample questions and other materials regarding the test. I asked my local college if there were books that I could check out, and I asked my colleagues if they had any resources. All turned out to be invaluable in assisting me to accomplish my goal.

Christian

## DO YOUR RESEARCH

Once you understand what is required of you, begin researching some of the school districts in your area. When looking for a corporate organization to work for, you scrutinized every aspect of their culture, vision, and mission. You wanted to know whether they were a good fit for you and you were a good fit for them. Working in education is no different. School districts and the individual schools themselves all have their own way of doing things; make sure that your goals and expectations match the culture of the school where you would like to teach.

Most schools in a division may allow you to visit and observe a classroom. You should request a meeting with the principal or a seasoned teacher to get a feel for the classroom environment. This is especially true if you are going into the classroom before you have begun a student teaching assignment.

During this visit, you should observe how a teacher interacts with her students. You want to study how she implements instructional strategies, transitions from one activity to another, and how she builds relationships with the students that she teaches.

In addition, focus your attention on how the teacher manages her classroom. In short, you need to

*Sticky Note: You want to study how the teacher implements instructional strategies, transitions from one activity to another, and builds relationships with the students that she teaches.*

*Sticky Note: To differentiate instruction, the educator will use a variety of strategies and methods to teach students of varying levels of readiness, while actively engaging them in the process.*

observe how the educator keeps all of their students on task and focused, as well as how she handles behavioral issues and students with disabilities.

During your observation, look for how the teacher tailors her instruction to the individual students. You may notice that some students need more or less information than the curriculum offers. More specifically, how does she engage the students using differentiated instruction?

To differentiate instruction, the educator will use a variety of strategies and methods to teach students of varying levels of readiness, while actively engaging them in the process. The instruction will cater to individual needs, while the students are working as a group, in small groups, in pairs, or independently.

## OTHER AREAS OF INTEREST

The topics listed below are briefly discussed here and in more detail throughout the book. Other areas of interest for potential educators may be benefits, tuition reimbursement, hours, and pay scale. Most of this information can be found on the school district's website. For example, some school districts will list the current or prior year's pay scales on their websites.

School divisions normally offer comprehensive insurance plans that you can opt to participate in. Additionally, you will find that many of the national and local teacher associations have insurance benefits as well. If you are a member of any of these associations, research their plan options and select the one that best fits your needs.

They will also list any benefits you may be entitled to, including how much the district will give in tuition assistance and list professional developments that are provided and/or allowed. The Internet is a great tool that can assist you in making an informed choice about what best fits your needs.

Many school divisions offer some type of educational reimbursement depending on the division's budget. The benefit from district to district can vary greatly. You may also find help for tuition through the Department of Education for your state. Your school division may have a list of what is available from the Department of Education, or you can contact them directly to get more information and requirements.

If you decide to teach in a national critical shortage area, you may qualify for the federal teach grant. This grant can pay for a portion, or all, of your education, if you commit to teaching in one of the critical shortage areas for a certain number of years. A critical shortage area is an area where there are not enough teachers for an identified subject in a specific area of the state. Bilingual education, mathematics, science, and special education are areas that have had shortages in the past.

Be aware that, although science may be a shortage in one area, this might not be the case throughout your entire state. Check your state's Department of Education website or the teach grant website for a current list of shortage areas. For more information on the teach grant, visit the Federal Student Aid website at www.studentaid.ed.gov.

If part of your decision is based on hours, ensure that this topic is addressed during your school visit or during the interview process. You want to have a clear understanding of the commitment that this position entails. Teaching is not only being in the classroom, but keep in mind there are several other factors that can cause you to have an extended day.

Some of these include faculty meetings, grading papers, parent conferences, late buses, and other duties that may be assigned such as bus duty or after-school detention. You may also be required to complete reports needed by the administration or set up/break down the classroom for the next activity or day.

Once you have done your research, you will have to complete your application process and submit it to the school districts for which you are applying. You may also want to find out who is hiring for your area of interest, call that staff person to introduce yourself, and ask about the requirements.

## THE INTERVIEW

When a school division calls you to come in for an interview, treat it just like you would treat any corporate position interview. Come prepared. Preparation can be the key to your success. School divisions are looking for people who know what they are doing, knowledgeable, have great communication skills, and love children. They want to know that you can meet the needs of every child in the classroom. They

*Sticky Note: Interviewers want to know that you can meet the needs of every child in the classroom.*

also want to know that you can handle challenging situations, when they arise, with professionalism and poise.

*On the Front Lines:*

When recruiting teachers from the business sector, I look first for their ability to market themselves as it relates to the building of relationships with children. Students perform best for individuals who reflect a high level of care and concern, which is balanced with high expectations. A large majority of the interview process focuses on *how* the interviewee responds to questions which relate to specific content areas (English, mathematics, science, and social science).

The interviewee must be knowledgeable about each content area to be taught, but above all else, understand how to deliver the instruction. Persons who are interested in teaching must be able to convey instruction in a manner in which the students can truly connect to the concept.

Williams

Even if you do not have any classroom experience, show them that you can do the job. Do your research and be able to explain what you would do when you are faced with students who are at different levels of readiness. Use the wealth of knowledge that you gained through your research and education process to impress those who are interviewing you. The school is their business, and they want those who are mindful, knowledgeable, and know how to make the business successful.

*On the Front Lines:*

First, administrators are looking for competent and committed persons who have a genuine love for children. The essential characteristics include integrity, honesty, a strong work ethic, going beyond the required duties, morally upright, and inner satisfaction. Administrators look for teachers who teach because it brings them an incredible feeling of satisfaction knowing they are contributing positively to the futures of others.

If a teacher doesn't have this inner satisfaction, and does not enjoy what they do, they'll never be able to make lasting impressions in their students' minds.

Passion has great impact, and this is something that all great teachers must have.

Hall-Lane

This is not only an interview for the school district to find an exceptional educator, but an opportunity for you to interview the school district. This position of employment should be a benefit to all parties involved. You should benefit from working for a school district that takes care of its teachers and students.

The school's culture should be a place where you, as well as the students, can flourish and grow. It should be a place where you feel supported throughout the many difficult tasks that you will have to complete.

The school district's expectation of you should be that of a dedicated and skilled educator who can be an instrumental part of the implementation of their educational plans and goals. The school district and your students should find that you are dependable and versatile in rendering a quality education to students. You have an understanding of what it takes to be successful and you make adjustments when needed.

Each school receives feedback on how they have performed through Adequate Yearly Progress (AYP). You should be aware of what these scores are and mean for your school. These scores represent the school division and/or a specific school's report card. The scores reflect student performance, in core subject areas, broken down by subject and groups.

These scores tell whether the school has met the expectation set by the Elementary and Secondary Education Act or No Child Left Behind Act. This progress report not only covers student performances but also issues such as safety, dropout rates, and highly qualified teacher data. This information can tell you what subjects and groups have been successful and which ones need improvement.

Armed with this information, you should ask your interviewer about their AYP scores and how they plan to improve their student achievement based on the data provided within the report card. Ask them what their opportunities and strengths are, and how you can play a part in improving these areas of weakness as well as maintaining the areas of strength.

Be prepared to explain why you feel qualified to help them achieve their goals. Once you have answered their questions and asked all of your own, review your understanding of what you heard and evaluate your options. Ensure that this is a place where you can grow and be a part of a culture that is not only there to achieve the best scores but also cares about the students being taught.

This should not have to be said, but some of us need reminders. Dress appropriately for your interview. In many corporate situations, you were required to represent the company in a way that would exemplify the company's success. Teachers are professionals, and you need to display your professionalism not only during the interview but even after you have been assigned to a position.

There is much to consider when embarking on this new career path. The professionals in this field must have a clear understanding of the requirements in order to make an informed decision about switching careers. Education, student teaching, types of licensure, and benefits are all critical pieces of information when you are considering a career in teaching.

If you decide that this profession is for you, do your research. Get as much knowledge of how to manage your classroom, your time, and your strategies for teaching before you enter this environment. The more you know, the better the transition will be.

*On the Front Lines:*

In 2003, I decided to switch careers and become a teacher. At the time, I was an executive assistant and a part-time art appreciation teacher at a local university. Prior to that, I was the Coordinator of Museum Operations at a small historic museum. When funding for my teaching position was gone, I decided to leave the university and pursue public education teaching because I love young people and I love teaching about art.

During the months that I was taking classes and the Praxis tests, I accepted a long-term substitute position to teach art at a middle school. Even though I had spent years as an elementary school volunteer, PTA officer, and substitute teacher, I was totally unprepared for the classroom nine years later. It was like culture shock.

I thought, wow, this will be a great opportunity for me to spend a few months getting to see how it will be to teach younger students in my field. My degree is in Art History, and this would help me decide which grade level I would like to teach. I thought surely it won't be difficult to teach art to children.

Boy, was I wrong. The first day I walked into the classroom, I felt like I was hit by a ton of bricks. No one prepared me for what I was about to come face to face with. No one told me that the reason the teacher had taken a leave of absence was because she had a nervous breakdown due to her teaching experience.

This, of course, meant that her classes were totally out of control. I was dumbfounded and in a state of shock at the lack of respect, the unruliness, and the disinterest the students displayed. Students brought their own deck of cards and proceeded to play adult card games. They refused to stop.

Students used inappropriate language as easily as they took a breath of air. I thought, okay, I can handle this. I am an intelligent adult and have raised two kids. I know discipline and how to establish rules. So in a few days, everything will be under control. NOT!

They ignored my presence; they disrespected me, their peers, and themselves. They were confrontational, and I sent students to the office for reprimand all day, every day. And they were sent back to the classroom without receiving any consequences from the administration.

This went on for a couple of weeks . . . students out of control, no help from school administrators, no help from other teachers because they were going through the same thing, and no help from parents. I felt alone and helpless. I went home every day and cried. I kept hoping things would get better so I stayed.

Underwood

# 2

# The Contract

Your interview went well and you were offered a position. With your contract in hand you are now one step closer to the classroom. As with any other contract, this is a legally binding agreement. The terms will list the requirements and responsibilities expected of you. We live in a society where we are quick to sign and slow to read.

The terms of this contract will dictate how you will spend the next nine to eleven months of your life. Please make sure you read and understand this agreement in its entirety. Some terms of your contract will discuss the amount of hours and days that you are required to work, your salary amount and any bonuses,

*Sticky Note: Please make sure you read and understand this agreement in its entirety.*

your responsibility to care for students, requirements of licensure, and terms to terminate the agreement.

*On the Front Lines:*

One item that really stood out in my contract was the fact that I was required to perform emergency and non-emergency health-related services to the students to which I am assigned. I am a special education teacher, and some of my students have medical issues that may require some sort of assistance.

This requirement was unnerving to me because I signed my contract not fully aware of what this term really meant for me. Although I had been certified in child CPR a few times in my life, it is not something that I use or practice regularly. Therefore, I was very uncomfortable with the thought of the possibility of performing it. CPR training has not been mentioned by the school district, so in a true emergency, I am not sure that I can fulfill this portion of the agreement.

Christian

As stated in chapter 1, you want to be very clear on what is expected of you. Go into this assignment with your eyes open and your mind prepared for the opportunities that lie ahead, opportunities that will challenge you and those that will enrich the life of someone else.

## HOURS

Be completely aware that this is not a nine-to-five job. Your contract may state that you are to start at 8:00 a.m. and end at 3:00 p.m., but most likely that is not

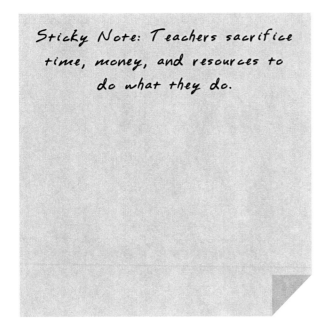

Sticky Note: Teachers sacrifice time, money, and resources to do what they do.

how your day will unfold. Teaching is a commitment that takes you well beyond those time boundaries. There may be days that you are engrossed in preparation or postwork all day, literally.

Teachers sacrifice time, money, and resources to do what they do. The amount of work that must be accomplished can be overwhelming. You may need to complete a project for administration, grade papers to give students feedback in a timely manner, and complete lesson planning at the same time. This can be very discouraging. This position requires a great deal of organization and time, especially in the beginning.

*On the Front Lines:*

I was under the impression that being a teacher meant I reported to work by 8:00 a.m. and if I was really lucky, I would leave by 2:30 p.m. To my surprise and despair, I spent several hours at school, after the "school day" had ended. On top of that, I regularly took home what I did not finish at school, to complete in the evenings and on weekends.

I dedicated most Saturday and Sunday afternoons to lesson planning. This was disappointing because one of my reasons for the career change was to spend more time with my family, but I ended up spending

much less time with them. This was true my first year and subsequent years due to changing grade levels. Parts of the position do get better as the years go by. For example, established lesson plans may only have to be tweaked instead of created from scratch.

Nevertheless, the responsibility is still great. As a teacher you are a lifelong learner and a collaborator. What may have worked three years ago may need to be revamped for your current class. Students one year may lean toward one learning style, and the next year you must figure out how to reach students with different learning styles.

You also have other issues that may cause you to be in your classroom beyond your contractual time. For instance, you may have students that arrive and leave the school via different forms of transportation. Sometimes buses are late due to various reasons, which cause you to have to stay with your students until it arrives.

Christian

## OTHER DUTIES AS ASSIGNED

In addition to the many tasks that you are required to complete in your classroom, there are additional tasks that may be required. In the corporate world, this is described as "other duties as assigned." Your school division is responsible for the students that they service and must ensure that the students are in a safe, organized environment. Thus, there is a need for staff to monitor the bus loops, hallways, and cafeterias, as well as organize committees to assist with morale, events, discipline, and the like.

You may be assigned to one or more of these duties that may require your presence on a daily basis or require you to participate periodically in a given task. In addition, there seems to be a constant need for volunteers for one task or another. Be prepared to respond to a request to volunteer throughout the school year.

Be careful not to overextend yourself. As a new teacher your plate will be pretty full, so although you may want to be a part of the exciting events that your school is hosting, it may not be expedient for you. Pace yourself; when you are overextended something

Sticky Note: Pace yourself; when you are overextended something is bound to fall through the cracks.

is bound to fall through the cracks. You do not want that "something" to be your students. They deserve your best. *The First-Year Teacher's Survival Guide, by Julia Thompson,* states, "It is common for a new teacher to agree to an extra duty but later find that the time required by the additional responsibility makes it difficult to be an effective classroom teacher."

*On the Front Lines:*

To me being a teacher means being part of a profession that makes a difference in society as a whole. It is the most rewarding job to have. To witness students I taught, succeed at the goal of graduating from high school is satisfying. But there are some drawbacks to teaching. Some of the things I didn't take into consideration were the long hours invested on grading papers, completing progress reports, and—don't forget—the after-school activities.

Goode

## TERMS

Your contract will be stated in general terms, as most everyone in the school division signs a similar contract. That being said, pay and other benefits may be negotiable, especially if there is a high need for your field of expertise. There may also be an opportunity

to receive a bonus that could or could not be tied to a contingency in the contract.

The contract can automatically renew or it could be a document that has to be renewed each school year. To ensure that schools are staffed for the next school year, most school divisions want to know your intent for teaching while you are still fulfilling your commitment during the current school year.

This allows the school district to make any adjustments to personnel early and allows you to know that you have a job for the upcoming school year before you leave for summer break. It also means that if you are planning to move from one division to another, you will have to apply sooner rather than later.

Another factor to note is the school division may eliminate the need for your current position. If this is the case, you may be able to find a job in the same division. This may mean that you will have to teach at a different grade level in order to maintain a position with that school division. You may request a transfer, or it may be written in your contract that you can be moved to any school within the division by the discretion of the school division.

A school district may be required to inform their staff, by a certain date, whether they have a position

Sticky Note: A school district may be required to inform their staff of whether they have a position for the upcoming school year by a certain date.

for the upcoming school year. Normally, this date is in the spring. These projections for jobs may be based on a budget that has not been set in stone. If that is the case, some teachers who may have been told that their positions were eliminated may find that they will be offered a contract, if they have not already found a new one.

Of course, if you are told that your job may be eliminated, you want to make sure that you explore all of the options. Be open to seeking a position in a school district where you have previously applied or one that may be in an area that you have not yet considered.

You also need to be aware that lost time at school for weather or any other cause may extend the school term. If you plan to take a vacation immediately after the school year ends, you may want to give yourself a little cushion to ensure that you can leave on the designated day.

The last day of school does not necessarily mean the last day of school for you. There may be required teacher work days that you must complete. Teacher work days, as well as student holiday/vacation days may serve as make-up days. You should keep this at the forefront of your mind when you are scheduling personal appointments. Your appointments may be affected if the day is used as a make-up day. In some cases, these decisions are made without much notice.

There may be laws that dictate the amount of time that teachers and students are required to spend in school. These make-up days ensure that the commitment is fulfilled.

*Sticky Note: The last day of school does not necessarily mean the last day of school for you.*

Obtaining your contract is just the first hurdle in your journey to educate students. This major step in the process must be entered into with care. Ensure that you have a thorough understanding of the terms and conditions of your contract. Be prepared to spend long days dedicated to becoming the best educator you can be.

At the same time, know your limits and do not bite off more than you can chew. This career change will be time consuming and challenging but has many great benefits like seeing students, who were otherwise left to fail, succeed. And do not forget those well-deserved breaks!

# 3

# Training

As stated in chapter 1, you can start your career by completing all of the required courses and hours of student teaching or by taking an alternative route that requires a bachelor's degree and no student teaching at all. Teachers who start with the latter have most likely selected this route because it is the quickest route to teaching in a classroom.

In most states you can receive provisional, emergency, or temporary licenses, which all function in a like manner. These licenses allow school districts to fill positions that fall under one of the critical shortage or emergency areas. Critical shortage areas may vary within a state depending on the need. Some critical shortage areas are science, mathematics, special education, and middle and high school social science.

Because these areas have such a high demand, some licensure requirements may be waived or you may be able to meet these requirements while you function as a teacher in the classroom. For example, in Virginia, a person may enter into the special education field with a bachelor's degree and one class that discusses the legal aspects of teaching special education. In addition, they are required to complete the remainder of their coursework within three years.

If you are entering this field with the minimum licensing requirements for becoming a teacher in your state, brace yourself. You will be expected to function just like a veteran counterpart on the first day of school. Yes, you did read that correctly! Your eyes are not deceiving you. You have not taught a day in your life and you will be expected to do so on the first day.

Sticky Note: The National Center for Education's statistics list which states' policies waive selected teacher certification requirements as well as which states allow teachers to obtain a provisional, temporary, or emergency license. The list is available at http://nces.ed.gov/pubs2003/2003020.pdf

The task is daunting but not impossible. Your preparation and seeking out formal and informal mentors will help you through the process. Learn the material first, so that you can teach the material well.

## CORPORATE VS. SCHOOL DISTRICTS

When you think about training from a corporate standpoint, you may imagine going through a training regimen that includes time in a classroom as well as some on-the-job training. Many corporations spend millions of dollars ensuring that the associates that they release into their corporate structure are trained and well prepared for the position at hand. This training goes beyond any college preparation that one may have achieved. This is not the case in the education field.

*On the Front Lines:*

It takes about three years to get an investigator fully functional at the "flawless" level. In helping employees get to that level of expertise, there is ongoing indoctrination. This includes providing them with a policy and procedure manual outlining how we do things, and how we expect processes to be performed the same way every time so that our clients anticipate certain valuable outcomes every time.

We bring in business leaders from the community on a regular basis to discuss concepts related to leadership, branding, accountability, and other areas important to companies seeking to compete at a high level. Our employees, at every level, get an opportunity to represent our company at various community events. We believe this enhances their sense of being a part of a special organization.

We assist our employees in setting professional and personal goals at the beginning of the year, and help them put together action plans, along with target dates, for accomplishing those goals. Their goals are reviewed on a quarterly basis. Finally, our employees attend one major training session on some aspect of their job every year. This usually involves traveling to a tourist destination, and incorporates some recreation time as a bonus for their hard work.

They are also required to design a continuous improvement program of their own, such as taking a class at a local college or an online course. These courses must have some relationship to their professional environment.

Clinton Investigation, LLC

*On the Front Lines:*

Training is the key to our success. We have a comprehensive training curriculum which focuses on all of the adult learning styles and is geared towards team building and individual development. The current curriculum is approximately seven weeks in length. This includes five weeks of classroom facilitation and two weeks of OJT (On-the-Job Training).

It usually takes about six–eight months after training for a new hire to feel completely comfortable with everything they've been taught. They have real-time coaching and feedback opportunities on a daily basis. Expectations are set early, and performance is tracked to ensure the success of the candidates.

New facilitators also go through a Facilitation 101 class, in which a seasoned trainer covers basic facilitation techniques. The trainer is then paired with a seasoned trainer to watch the class facilitated from beginning to end. The next phase of the on-boarding process is co-facilitation. In this phase the new trainer is paired with a seasoned trainer. This will allow the seasoned trainer to help guide the new trainer as well as provide opportunities for "in the moment" coaching and support.

The last phase of the on-boarding process is when the new trainer will have the opportunity to facilitate their own class. After the class the participants will complete level 1 surveys and the training manager will coach the new trainer with the feedback found in the survey.

Boots Corporate Trainer

As a teacher entering into this field, you should expect to receive limited or no additional training such as on-the-job training or shadowing another person. These types of training regimens are not as organized or detailed in this field. This does not mean that there is nothing available to you.

Most school divisions have some sort of mentoring program or new teacher induction program, but these programs do not explain all the jargon or requirements in a manner that is timely or expedient. Many of the obstacles that you may face will make you feel alone and/or without direction.

*On the Front Lines:*

My first year of public school teaching as a career switcher was indeed more of a learning experience for me than my students. Our mentoring program was not a real program, and even though my mentor helped, there was so much more that I didn't get help with. I never got a tour of the school, so I had to ask or figure out where things were. Each school administrator has his/her own philosophy of how to run a school, which is okay until you teach at two different schools. I didn't feel like I belonged at either.

Underwood

*Sticky Note: As a teacher you are expected to come in ready to teach, despite your level of experience or classroom knowledge.*

Many corporate executives give you at least a six-month timeframe to grasp all that is required in the position that you are filling. This time allows you to get an understanding of what is expected, how you should best handle situations and clients that you serve, where to go for help, who has the final authority in any matter, how to complete all needed paperwork, and the daily ins and outs of the position.

During this process management will normally check on your progress. You will have either an informal or formal meeting to discuss what you are doing right and areas where you can improve. For the most part, you have a good idea of where you stand.

As a teacher you are expected to come in ready to teach, despite your level of experience or classroom knowledge. You are required to function as an experienced teacher. You are let loose to either sink or swim from the very first day of school; if your actions do not cause pandemonium with the parents, you may never be told what you are doing right or what opportunities you may have.

You will most likely be left to your own devices. If this is the case, lean on your mentor or other teachers to guide you through the process. The lack of help may not be intentional. There are many factors that may prevent you from receiving the help that you need.

There are so many things that must be accomplished in a school day that others may not have time to help. It is difficult for the administration and your teammates to complete the required work and issues that emerge throughout the day. Helping a fellow worker may be where their heart is, but it just may not be feasible for them.

*On the Front Lines:*

During my first year of teaching, I was trained how to communicate with parents and handle their concerns during parent conferences in April. This was very frustrating for me because we had completed all of our scheduled parent conferences for the year. This information would have been more helpful if it was presented near the beginning of the school year instead of the end.

Christian

This process can be very exasperating, but do not let it fester and become a negative point for you. When the opportunity presents itself, share your experience and how translating some of the corporate methods into this field could be beneficial to all involved.

## PROFESSIONAL DEVELOPMENT

Professional development is one of the methods that the school system uses to train and develop its educators. You may be mandated to complete a certain number of professional development hours to maintain your certification. These hours can be obtained through workshops, conferences, coursework, and teacher-to-teacher initiatives.

Furthermore, these development opportunities can give you ideas and advice on classroom management and effective teaching strategies, but depending on the district and the funding available, these may be hard to come by. You can find these development opportunities by contacting your state's Department of Education website, or your district or other local district's websites, as well as one of the many teacher associations available for membership.

When these professional development opportunities are offered, you will occasionally be subject to

*Sticky Note: Professional development is one of the methods that the school system uses to train and develop its educators.*

topics that have nothing to do with your current job. The training will focus on a grade or subject that you do not teach. While it may seem like a waste of time, several teachers have chosen to teach different grades and subjects after building on their endorsement areas, or teachers may have been asked to teach a different grade by their school district. These training sessions may come in handy at a later date, so take good notes and file them away for later retrieval.

## OBSERVATIONS

In addition to your lack of experience and training, you must expect and be prepared for the unannounced and announced visits to your classroom. Depending on your comfort level and confidence, these visits can range from "no big deal" to "I want my mommy." The regimen or scheduling of these visits will vary from school to school. There are some teachers who have been observed once during their first year, while there are others who may feel like the principal is always in their classroom.

The best way to handle these potentially nerve-racking experiences is to view the observation as an opportunity to receive feedback. We may not always want to hear feedback, but it can be used as a tool for growth. Feedback is like a vitamin; when taken properly it can cause you to perform at an even higher level.

In a corporate environment, feedback was a part of life. You had, at the very least, an annual review where you discussed your progress and your challenges and brainstormed to devise new goals for the following year. You may have also experienced the daily and/or weekly morning meeting where you discussed your daily or weekly goals to make sure that your group was on the same page.

Preparation for the observation will make it flow more smoothly and may lessen your discomfort. You should always have your lesson plans prepared and available for the observer to view. During the lesson, you should exhibit that you understand the needs and learning styles of your students. This should be something that the observer sees through your use of materials and differentiated instruction.

The points of your lesson should be clear and easy to understand, reiterating important information. You should be professional and show that you understand where students are and you know how to get them all to the same destination. Observers want to see your students engaged in the learning process, but do not panic if one student is not doing exactly what you want

*Sticky Note: Feedback is like a vitamin; when taken properly it can cause you to perform at an even higher level.*

him to do. The observer knows that this environment may not show a perfect picture.

*On the Front Lines:*

On more than one occasion I had an observer in my room and a few of my kids were out of their seats, playing with something, speaking out of turn, or having a meltdown. I was thinking to myself, "This is a disaster. Why did they show up now?! My lesson earlier went so well." I knew that I would receive some sort of negative feedback but that was far from the case. They understood that children will be children and they reminded me that it was age-appropriate behavior.

The few times that a suggestion was made it was just that, a suggestion. Something to the effect of, "Have you thought about trying this activity?" or "What if you had done this after your initial introduction?" I learned not to stress and say, "They will see what they see." As long as I prepare and deliver my lesson the way I normally do, there is nothing to worry about.

Christian

Normally, within a few days of your observation you will meet the observer to discuss her findings. This, in turn, gives you the opportunity to find out exactly what is expected of you, though you may want to know these expectations in advance. It also gives you a chance to ask questions or voice some of your own concerns. In essence, it will let you know what you should be striving for, adding, or changing in the classroom environment.

The feedback can help you create goals for yourself throughout the year. Many school districts require that you complete a professional growth plan. This plan is normally completed twice a year. In this plan you must develop goals, design a process for implementation, as well as discuss the results of the growth plan. Your feedback from an observation can assist you in completing this document. A sample professional growth plan is located in appendix E of this book.

Some of the questions that you may consider when writing a growth plan are as follows:

1. How do you plan to meet the goals of your school and the standards of learning for your state?

2. How will this plan be implemented?
3. How does the plan impact the academic performance of the students?
4. Did you meet the goals and objectives set? Why or why not? (This question will most likely be answered when you update the growth plan near the end of the year.)
5. List any professional developments or classes taken that can be used toward licensure or make you more marketable. Make sure that you list these especially if they help you achieve your listed goals.

## NEW TEACHER WEEK

The first introduction to what the school division has to offer in the way of training is typically referred to as New Teacher Week. Some divisions require the "new" teacher to come to the school a week or so before everyone else. This allows the "newbie" time to become acclimated to the school division's way of doing things, the general policies, procedures, and benefits that the school has to offer, as well as some extra time to set up their classroom.

You may meet some of the teams that will do the new teacher training, your principals, and the support staff. Take note of the personnel you meet; you may

Sticky Note: Take note of the personnel you meet; they may be instrumental throughout the school year.

need to contact some of these individuals about different issues. This list will be instrumental to you over the next year.

You want to get to know those who can help you throughout the year. The secretary, janitors, maintenance crew, and computer technicians should become your new best friends. These individuals can make the school year run more smoothly.

The principals of your school will most likely meet with you and go over individual school policies, general expectations (attendance, contact information, how to complete general paperwork, etc.). They may introduce you to some of the staff and show you to your classroom. Do not expect an overwhelming amount of attention at this time because the principals are normally dealing with many aspects of the school, in preparation for the return of the staff as well as the students for the first day of school.

While you have your principal's attention, ask about training and whether you have an option to sit in on a few other classes for observation purposes. This is also something good to do when you are beginning to consider this profession or a particular school division. This does not mean that you will not start in your own classroom, but it will give you an opportunity to see how someone else may handle different situations.

There are some new teachers who will get the benefit of observing another more seasoned teacher during their student teaching experience, but if you are not one of those fortunate new teachers, ask for and use these resources as quickly as possible.

**NEW TEACHER PROGRAM**

Some schools and/or districts have new teacher induction programs. These programs may require you to meet before or after school once or twice a month to receive additional training. Normally these training sessions will go toward your professional development requirements. The topics discussed may not have anything to do with your grade level or subject.

Districts may require that all new teachers attend these sessions whether they are applicable or not. Again, take it in stride; you never know which way

your teaching path will lead you and you may have to revisit your notes and use the strategies presented for your new assignment.

A new teacher program provides training on some of the situations that you may encounter the first year. It could include topics ranging from classroom management, to how to prepare students for a test, to dealing with uncooperative parents. As with professional development, some topics can be right on target to what you need in your classroom, while others may not apply to you at all. You want to find out how organized and well developed these sessions are and come in with the expectation that some of these sessions will not be geared toward what you do but may help the new teacher sitting next to you.

These sessions may include new teachers from the entire division that teach a spectrum of grade levels. As you may know, a kindergarten teacher's needs are very different from someone teaching ninth grade. Even with the differences, there are topics that are common to all.

During these sessions come prepared with questions. If you know that parent conferences are coming up, ask about what to do even if it's not on the agenda. A teacher's time is valuable; so make these meetings worth your while.

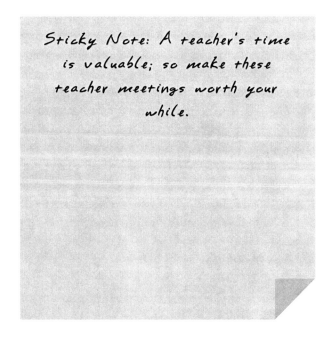

Sticky Note: A teacher's time is valuable; so make these teacher meetings worth your while.

There will be times throughout the school year where you will not know what questions to ask. There are some situations that will not come up until you need the answer or the solution to the problem. Do not let this frustrate you. This happens to the best teachers; contact your mentor, informal mentor, or administration for guidance on how to handle the issue.

## MENTORS

Before you begin the new school year, you may also want to find out who will be your assigned mentor. Your mentor will most likely be a teacher with all of his credentials who receives a stipend to help you throughout the school year. Find out how accessible the mentor is, ask if he will permit you to sit in on some of his classes, and find out what grades and subjects he teaches.

Note that you may only have this mentor the first year of teaching; many districts do not plan for a formal mentor beyond this time. If so, depend on informal mentors to get you through situations that may not have come up during your first year.

You can receive a very organized mentor who has a wealth of information to share or someone who is looking to receive the extra pay with as little effort as possible. Either way, do not rely on this person as your sole resource. These individuals are trying to maintain planning for their own classrooms and life obligations; they will only be able to commit to a limited amount of time.

Mentors should be there to give you suggestions regarding lesson planning, parent communication, classroom management, and teaching strategies; assist in preparing individual educational plans (IEP) and IEP meetings (special education); keep you abreast of events, and so on. Hopefully your mentor is in the same building and you can just pop into her classroom as needed.

Mentor relationships can sometimes become strained due to mismatched personalities, work ethics, mindsets, or knowledge of the skill sets needed to prepare you for your grade level and subject. If there are issues that you cannot work out between the two of you, get administration involved or express your concerns to one of the new teacher trainers. You may be surprised; it could be a simple fix.

Even if your mentor is exceptional, there will be limits to how much he can help you. In all likelihood, your mentor has responsibilities of his own that must be accomplished. As a result, accessibility may be limited at a time when you feel that you need your mentor the most. In any case, you will need to know what other resources are available to you.

*On the Front Lines:*

Most people are more than willing to give you ideas and share resources with you. But, you must ask for these things! All teachers have so much going on with standards, tests, and paperwork that they don't realize that you need help. It isn't that they don't want to help you out as a new teacher. The just have so much going on that they don't realize that you need help.

Most veteran teachers remember how hard it was starting out, so they are more than willing to help you with what you need. Sometimes the challenge is figuring out what you need or what you want to do! The first year is overwhelming because you are in charge of so much and don't always know what you are doing since you are a rookie. The most important thing you can do is keep smiling and keep asking for help! The first year is the hardest. Each year after that gets easier as you gain more experience.

Ashley

If you are not assigned a mentor or your mentor is not accessible, keep your eyes open for informal mentors. When you meet teachers that say "if you need anything," make a note of who they are and take advantage of their offer. These informal mentors have a wealth of knowledge and experience; be sure to utilize it, especially if they have been in the system for a while.

*On the Front Lines:*

Teaching is a demanding job. It is stressful, physical, and can be an emotional roller coaster. Do not let yourself become overwhelmed. Ask for help if you

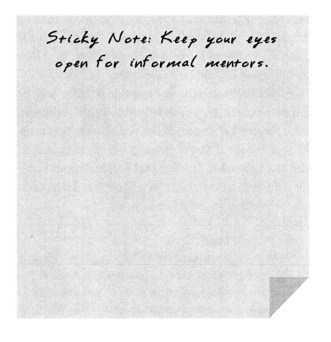

*Sticky Note: Keep your eyes open for informal mentors.*

need it and do not be afraid to admit that you may have done something incorrectly. Teaching, itself, is a learning process.

Cousins

As with any organization you are going to meet those who have been burned by administration, co-workers, parents, and students. Do not let their negative experience dictate how you choose to handle your students and the experiences that you may face. Listen to what the informal mentor has to offer, and apply the information that is helpful in the management of your classroom.

Beware: all that is offered may not be good for you. Use what is helpful and dispel the rest. Judge your colleagues, parents, and, most importantly, your students based on their own merit and not that of others. Bottom line: sift out what you can use and discard the rest.

*On the Front Lines:*

   As great a resource as veteran teachers may be, be careful to not let another person's opinion of a child (especially one whom you have not yet met) cause you to form a negative opinion of a child. Let the child make their own first impression.

Cousins

## COLLEAGUES

In most corporations, there is a "go-to" guy, someone who could help you find or lead you to the person with the answer to a problem. Schools are no different. You should make it a point to familiarize yourself with those who labor among you. Almost certainly, there are teachers who have knowledge on a specific topic and/or experience that you can draw from, and most of them are more than willing to help.

There are those who have a specific skill in working with computers, the projector, software, reports, or classroom management that can give you a course of action for whatever your problem may be. Even if the teacher you choose to ask does not know how to fix it, she may know who the "go-to" guy is.

Even with all of these prospects of gaining the knowledge you need, the delivery of anecdotes may not be timely. For instance, you may attend a professional development seminar on classroom management a month after a student has thrown a desk and hit another student in your class. You must prepare yourself as much as possible, ask questions, visit several classrooms, and observe the strategies used by different teachers. Seek out as many training opportunities that you can, get feedback, role play, and read books like this one.

*Sticky Note: Judge your colleagues, parents, and, most importantly, your students based on their own merit and not the opinions of others.*

# 4

# You're a Teacher Now

## MONEY

Ready, Set, Buy! Teachers can spend a substantial amount of money buying needed materials for their classrooms. It would be great to say that when you walk into your classroom everything you need will be right there for the asking. That is not the case for most teachers, especially with budget cuts. In many instances, teachers are left to their own devices to get the materials needed to set up their classrooms and teach their lessons.

School divisions may supply all to some of the books you need, but you may find in some divisions that you have to share or go without a teacher's edition manual, student books, workbooks, technology, and so forth. Although you are missing these items, you are still required to teach the standards of learning in these books. You may have to make copies (be careful of copyrighted material) or print items from the Internet to fill the deficit.

Remember, this is not every case. If you are lucky, you may get a budget at the beginning of the year allowing you to buy some of the everyday items needed. Some schools have a supply closet where you are able to request the items that you need. Find out from your principal whether this is an option for you. Even with a budgeted amount of money or use of a supply closet, be prepared to buy additional items for your classroom.

Many of the classrooms that you see nicely decorated and full of interesting objects were paid for out of the teacher's own funds. Teachers need to be resourceful. Keep your eyes and ears open for items that other teachers may not want and/or are giving away. There may be teachers who are retiring or changing jobs who are distributing some of their items.

If you are able to request items, prepare your list thoughtfully. Ensure you think about some of the projects that you may do and add these materials to your list. Really cute items are nice, but make certain you have the functional items first.

Fortunately, there are organizations out there that try to help teachers find sponsorship for the classroom. Two such organizations are Donors Choose (donorschoose.org) and Adopt-a-Classroom (adoptaclassroom.org). These organizations will allow you to post a message on their website and serve as your liaison. By using their pre-made flyers, you can ask parents, friends, and acquaintances for their support. These organizations also have donors that can decide on the spot to sponsor a project that you are proposing.

In addition, you can ask businesses for support. If you ask for support in these arenas, be prepared to hear "no" or that organizations already have "set" causes that they give to. Take comfort in knowing that among all of the businesses that decide not to support you, there are some that will. When soliciting this help, make sure that you know what items you need so that you can share those needs with whomever will listen.

*Sticky Note: You want your classroom to be a space that invites your students to explore the entire sphere of the subject you teach.*

You want your classroom to be a space that invites your students to explore the entire sphere of the subject you teach. You want them to feel that the atmosphere that you have prepared has no limitation on the things that they can achieve. The students should buy into what you are setting before them. You want them to feel that their exploration will be an adventure in the confines of a safe environment. It should be an environment where they can make mistakes and challenge their current thought process.

*On the Front Lines:*
I think the salary isn't bad for the amount of months we work. But I didn't think about the extra resources needed until I started teaching. I thought it was strange when my child's teacher asked for hand sanitizer or colored paper. Now I realize why they did this. All the extras they wanted come directly out of their family budget.

Goode

*On the Front Lines:*
No one prepared me for the lack of funds that would be available for supplies. When my supplies ran out, there was no money to buy more. I either paid out of pocket and/or asked parents and others to do-

nate certain supplies. Coming from a non-profit environment, I was hoping to not have to solicit anymore.

Underwood

## DECORATING YOUR ROOM

How you decorate or set up your classroom plays an important part in creating the atmosphere that you are trying to achieve. Your classroom should not be "busy" for the sake of having stuff on the walls. What you post should have a purpose. Julia Thompson, author of *The First-Year Teacher's Checklist*, shares, "Although your classroom décor should be attractive, the emphasis should be on creating an environment that teaches content."

Your bulletin boards, doors, and walls should be meaningful and interactive, a source that prompts discussion. These areas can be something that the students participate in creating. This will give them an area where students can express themselves and put into practice some of what they are learning. Debbie Miller, author of *Teaching with Intention*, notes, "Classroom environments are organic—they grow as we do." You should post reminders for things like the rules of the classroom, scientific method steps, or basic information for a particular subject.

*Sticky Note: Your bulletin boards, doors, and walls should be meaningful and interactive, a source that prompts discussion.*

Using these resources, you can poll your students and find out what they like or dislike about a topic, book, or discussion. There are many ways you can engage your students by simply displaying something on the walls. Jeanna Bryer's article, "Rewards Not Working?" explains, "It's important to experience a sense of autonomy, a feeling that we are initiators of much of what we do."

These items do not have to be expensive pre-made or pre-fabricated ideas. They can be items that you collaborate with your students or other educators on and put together yourself. You may find that some of the best ideas come out of brainstorming sessions with whomever you choose. Consider even giving bulletin boards to groups of students as an ongoing project, as a way to give them a sense of ownership on what and how they learn.

**SEATING ARRANGEMENTS**

In addition to the items brought into your classroom, your desk arrangement is very important. From the beginning, keep the mindset that this is a fluid design; it can be altered or changed at any time. You want to make sure that the desks are arranged for optimal learning. The arrangement should allow you to have sight of all of your students and your students' sight of you and the board. This may mean that for a portion of the day you have one arrangement that can easily be converted to another.

Arranging the desks requires that you know your students. Of course, the first few weeks you will have a limited amount of insight, but make notes and adjust your plan as necessary. You'll want to ensure that students are in the best seat to optimize their learning experience. You do not want to place a student who has a visual or hearing impairment in an area of the classroom that will cause her to struggle. Also, take into account that you may need to place someone who may be wheelchair bound or who may require extra help with instruction.

A poorly designed classroom will cause an environment to have disruptions and behavioral management

*Sticky Note: A poorly designed classroom will cause an environment to have disruptions and behavioral management issues that can and will affect the quality of learning.*

issues that can and will affect the quality of learning. Do not just have a plan but commit your plan to paper; that way you are also sharing your insight with those who may have to cover your classroom.

**CENTERS**

Setting up your classroom to include centers allows you to work with students one-on-one or in small groups. It also gives students an opportunity to explore new concepts individually, collaboratively in pairs, or in small groups.

You can start with a few centers and include more activities throughout the year. For example, you may not want to introduce a writing center at the beginning of the year because you may need to introduce prewriting standards before the students can begin to write. There are many centers that can be included throughout the school year. Writing, listening, math, or file folder games are just a few ways to incorporate this tool into your classroom.

This tool can bridge the gap for some students by engaging them in the learning process and providing extra practice of a specific concept or topic. It can also give you an opportunity to cross your curriculum. Your activities may include something that they learned in science but also incorporates reading, writing, and/or mathematic goals.

*On the Front Lines:*

One of the centers that has been a great success in my classroom is a clothesline that I set up near my cubbies. The clothesline has clothespins with capital letters written on each of them. The students have to match the lowercase letter flash card to the uppercase letter that is written on the clothespin. The class also uses the clothesline to match picture cards to their beginning, middle, and ending sounds. Depending on the task, the students work as pairs or individuals. This has proven to be helpful in getting my students with disabilities active in what has been taught.

Christian

## ORGANIZATION

It is just as important to maintain order and a flow to the paperwork in your classroom. Students will be completing paperwork throughout the day and bringing in assignments that were completed at home; all of these papers need a place to go. You should think about how you want students to turn in assignments.

You may want to set up baskets or trays that are labeled *homework, test, morning work,* or any additional task where you collect papers. These baskets do not necessarily have to be labeled; some teachers color code their baskets or trays. Either way, the use of the baskets and/or trays is a great tool for keeping you and your classroom organized. One of the benefits to having baskets and/or trays is that it allows students to turn in work without being disruptive to other classmates.

You could also set up folders or binders by individual students. This setup may eliminate students sitting idly with nothing to do. These folders could contain additional tasks to extend a lesson that has been taught. You can also set up baskets or file folders for work that has been graded and should be returned to students.

In addition, there will be forms that you will need to keep handy. Leave forms, receipts, new student pack-

ets, disciplinary forms, referrals, and nurse slips are a few. An efficient place for these forms can make your day run much smoother. You do not want to waste time trying to figure out where you saw them last. Organize these forms where you or someone who may be in your room can find them quickly.

*On the Front Lines:*

As a teacher, it is important to be as organized as possible. If you are prepared and organized, your students (most of them) will be as well. It's all about modeling!

Cousins

## SETTING THE TONE

Now that you have set up your classroom, plan to start off your year on the right foot by showing the students that you mean business. Students seem to always be up to the task of finding the pushovers. One of the basic needs of a child is to feel safe. They need to know that your classroom is a place where they are expected to learn and follow classroom procedures.

Set the tone at the beginning of the year for the way you would like to see it continue throughout the year. Save yourself from frustration later. Just like pitching

*Sticky Note: Set the tone at the beginning of the year for the way you would like to see it continue throughout the year.*

an idea in the boardroom, share your expectations with the students; do not expect them to know what you want. The book *180 Tips and Tricks for New Teachers* states, "If you tell your students that you are going to do something, then you had better do it or they will lose respect for you. The tone that you set can be instrumental in overcoming anxiety for everyone by establishing clear rules and boundaries."

Students need to know who is in charge. If you allow them to misbehave and do things that are against your rules, you are asking for trouble. It is not that you have to be a dictator, but you do have to be an enforcer, someone who consistently enforces the rules. When consistency is not in place, you will not get a consistent behavior response from your students. You will spend much more of your time trying to correct the response than instructing the students.

## RULES

You should have a basic idea of what rules you want for your classroom, but do not commit these rules to paper or any other signage. You want to include your students in as much of the rule-creating process as possible. It is better to have your students own the process than to be told what the process will be.

*Sticky Note: It is better to have your students own the process than be told what the process will be.*

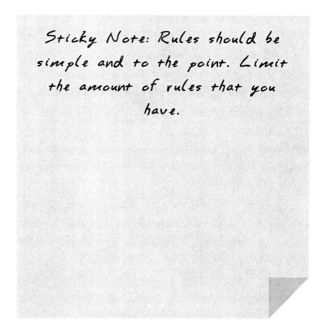

*Sticky Note: Rules should be simple and to the point. Limit the amount of rules that you have.*

Keep your rules simple and to the point. During a brainstorming activity, several ideas with the same theme may be brought up by the students. Guide the students into summarizing that idea and then add the one general rule to your posted list.

Limit the amount of rules that you have. Again, there are several rules that can encompass a multitude of trespasses. For example, "Respect everyone's possessions, feelings, and space" can cover how students treat one another and the teacher, keeping their hands to themselves, and not taking or destroying property that does not belong to them.

## PRACTICE WHAT YOU PREACH

Your students are watching you. So, as they say, you must practice what you preach. You cannot expect students to speak kindly to one another if you are always sarcastic and rude to them and your constituents. As much as you demand respect, you must show respect. If your actions do not line up with your words, your students will lose respect for your authority and put at risk your ability to manage your classroom effectively. *180 Tips and Tricks for New Teachers* notes, "Consistency in teaching basically means that your students know what to expect from you day to day."

## EMPOWER YOUR STUDENTS

One big theme in this chapter is getting your students involved in the process of learning. This is their educational journey, and whether they are a kindergartener or a senior in high school, they should be encouraged to take responsibility for their learning experience. You must stress that it is your job to give them the information but they have a job to do as well. They need to know it is also their job to learn what you are sharing with them.

The more they become part of the process, the better they will understand and retain the information. An active participant is bound to gain better insight than those who passively sit by and let the information come to them. Marilyn Gillespie wrote, "Purposeful and transparent learning builds on learners' prior knowledge and experiences to construct new knowledge."

You can empower them by assigning tasks. This not only helps with classroom management, but takes some of the burden of all classroom duties off of you. This will also give the student a sense of belonging and achievement. Many students love being responsible and sometimes are disappointed when it is not their week to do a particular job. Assign duties that inspire

the student to go beyond the passive stage and become active in the workings of their learning environment.

*On the Front Lines:*

I borrowed a great idea from one of my son's teachers. Instead of having a line leader or a paper collector, she has a president and a secretary. I love the fact that these names give the students more of a sense of pride in the job that they are responsible for.

Christian

## KNOW YOUR STUDENTS

Every year the needs of your students will change. What you did with your students one year may not work with your students the next year. You must be willing to make adjustments to keep up with the ever-changing needs of the students you teach. You have to be able to teach the same topic in a variety of ways and backtrack when necessary to ensure that your lessons are being understood by all of the students you teach. Teaching the same lesson employing a variety of methods is called *differentiation.*

Most of your students will not learn exactly the same way you learn. You will have to come out of your comfort zone and teach to the masses by saying

*Sticky Note: An active participant is bound to gain better insight than those that passively sit by and let the information come to them.*

*Sticky Note: Teaching the same lesson employing a variety of methods is called differentiation.*

or demonstrating the same information while communicating it on multiple levels. Knowing your students is one way to ensure that you are teaching and reaching them on these different levels. Melissa Kelly, the author of *180 Tips and Tricks for New Teachers*, suggests, "Each person has a particular learning style that is best for their intake and comprehension of new information."

You should know what they like and dislike, know what interests them, and incorporate some of those interests into your lessons. Differentiating does not necessarily mean flooding their senses with too many stimuli at one time. You may be able to teach something one way and go back and teach it another way.

At the beginning of the year, have your students and their parents complete an informational form explaining the students' likes, dislikes, strengths, and weaknesses. Have them periodically update these forms to keep your lessons fresh and appealing. The more you know about them, the more you can tailor your lessons to the interests of your students, engaging them in the learning experience. There is a sample of one such informational form, called the Insight Form, in appendix B of this book.

*On the Front Lines:*

The parents of my students always expressed gratitude because I took the time to find out about their child's likes and dislikes. I found ways throughout the year to incorporate their individual preferences. I did this by reading books about the topic, giving rewards that were tailored to their preferences, and tailoring assignments such as allowing them to do a report on their favorite book or animal.

Christian

# 5

# The Basics

## TIME MANAGEMENT

If you thought that you spent too much of your time in the office and you are ready for the days off and the short hours, you may be disappointed. This job, especially in the beginning, is very demanding. You will spend several hours working on the various tasks that are required of you, on and off the clock. That being said, you will need to learn how to manage your time effectively.

Many time management products focus on prioritizing your day. You need to make a list of all of the things that you need to accomplish and then rate them by importance. Everything that is not accomplished that day needs to be pushed to the next day. Use your time wisely. Consider what could be taken care of during the school day and strive to accomplish as much as possible.

There are things that you do that consume the time that you have, and there will be activities that must be done that are out of your control. You must work on your tasks daily, but make sure you have a broader perspective in mind. As a teacher, in a sense you are your manager. You must see beyond lesson planning, grading papers, and the like.

Schools often have assemblies for one reason or another that may interfere with what you have set to accomplish. You need to stay informed about what has been scheduled on the school's calendar and make sure your personal tasks do not conflict with those objectives of the school. Note that these events may be pushed back or up for one reason or another. The key is to be flexible.

Although you may stay informed with the latest happenings around the school, there may inevitably be something that will come up at the last minute that will need your attention. You may receive an email or a phone call midday, requesting information about a student from the school administration. They may want you to respond by the end of the school day. Do not panic! Make the adjustments and roll with the punches.

## SCHEDULE CHANGES

Throughout a school year you will find that it is jam-packed with assemblies, safety drills, and classes

Sticky Note: You must find ways to be creative and regain the missed time. Seize every opportunity to reinforce or teach a concept.

beyond the core curriculum. These extra activities will all be competing with the few hours that you have with your students. You may find that you cannot effectively complete your entire lesson, or if you are a resource teacher, it may hinder the progress of one or more of your groups.

You must find ways to be creative and regain the missed time. Seize every opportunity to reinforce or teach a concept. For example, if you are walking with your class to music or lunch, use that time to impart a standard or to practice what you have learned. Use the artwork or other items posted in the hallways as a tool to discuss an activity that you may have just accomplished.

*On the Front Lines:*

The hardest thing for me to do my first year was to manage my time and to get organized. Different people have their own ways of organizing themselves, but this method has worked for me. I have a small notebook where I keep all of my "to do" lists and reminders.

Each day, I divide the next page into three sections, "A," "B," and "C." In the "A" column, I list things that absolutely *have* to be done that day. I limit this list to five tasks. The "B" column has tasks that would be nice to get done, but are not crucial to the success of my day. Column "C" has tasks that need to get done eventually, but are not essential. At the end of my day, I look at which tasks I've crossed off. Then, before going home, I make a new list for the next day. The tasks in the "B" list end up of the "A" list, and the tasks in the "C" list end up on the "B" list. That way, I can keep track of all of the things that I eventually have to do, without stressing about getting it all done in one day.

Ashley

## LESSON PLANNING

A teacher who seems to have it all together is one who has taken the time to prepare. *180 Tips and Tricks for New Teachers* suggests that "when you are teaching, your goal should be to have students engaged from the moment they walk in your classroom to the moment they leave." Author Fred Jones, in *Tools for Teaching*,

put it this way: "Students enjoy learning when the process of instruction engages all of their senses." He goes on to say, "When students enjoy learning, teachers enjoy teaching."

Most school districts will give you the standards of learning and a pacing guide or chart that must be covered by your grade level for the year. The pacing guide will give you the objectives that should be taught to the students in a weekly or monthly format.

Some school districts provide readymade lesson plans to glean insight from. You can also obtain the standards of learning by visiting the Department of Education website for your state. You must then take these guidelines and decide how you will teach each topic throughout the year.

Your lesson plans can be very descriptive or very general. Some school districts require you to turn in your lesson plans and may have a format that you must abide by. There are staff members who like to plan together, and there are teachers who come up with their plans individually. Check with your principal, department head, or grade chair to find out how your school handles lesson planning.

Whatever format that your school system chooses, you need to ensure that your plans have enough detail

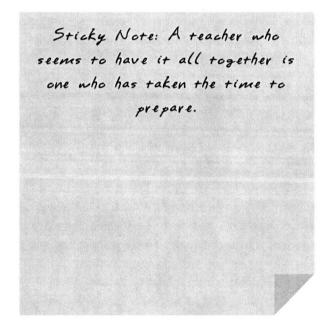

Sticky Note: A teacher who seems to have it all together is one who has taken the time to prepare.

for someone else to follow easily and make certain they meet the needs of your students. In addition, make sure that they are readily available. This may mean you will need to plan in advance and have them in your classroom. In case of an emergency, you want someone to be able to pick up where you left off without missing a beat.

Lesson plans vary in how much information is included in the actual plans. There are very detailed daily plans and weekly plans. Examples of both are located in the appendix D. The book *Timesavers for Teachers* also has many different sample plans and forms needed for the classroom. Some lesson plans follow a before, during, and after format. This format has been proven to yield great results according to research.

It provides a thorough plan of what you will do throughout the lesson, from beginning to end. It requires that you think about how you are going to introduce the topic, expand on that introduction, your use of technology, how you will close out the topic, and ultimately assess the students' knowledge. Before implementing any of the following steps, you should do a quick assessment of the material to get an understanding of what your students already know.

*Before:* This section focuses on how you get the students' attention and prepare them for the lesson you are about to teach. You are setting the atmosphere and preparing them for the journey they are about to embark on. You are introducing them to a new concept.

Remember that everyone is not starting from the same point, but the goal is to get them all to the finish line. Do not expect everyone to learn the material in the same way; be sure to differentiate. The lesson should make the students want to know more or apply what they have learned. Give them an opportunity to go beyond the lesson and find out more on the topic. Debbie Miller states in her book, *Teaching with Intention*, "I believe learning is maximized when the lessons I design are purposeful, interactive, and engaging with real-world application."

*During:* In this portion of your lesson plan, you are conveying the "meat" or the objective of your lesson. Your main point(s) should be clearly established, with background as well as supporting information. It is your job not only to feed the students the information but to make sure that they are eating what you have placed before them.

You can do this by modeling or showing them how you would address the topic (talking through the process is one example). You can do this by yourself first and then involve your group. Actively engaged students become intrigued with what they are learning. While they are engaged, encourage them to explore the possibilities.

*After:* Now that you have gotten their attention and delivered the main course, seal the deal. Exercise what they know or have learned by providing some type of assessment activity. This will provide you with data that can determine whether the lesson was successful and if the students understood what was being taught or whether you need to regroup, re-teach, and/or try another angle.

If you need to regroup, re-teach, and/or try another angle, use the information that you have collected as a tool to figure out what you need to do next. This step is crucial to determining whether to stay where you are or move on.

Do not stop there. You can make more connections to your lesson by extending the lesson beyond

Sticky Note: Introduce your topic, convey your main points clearly, offer a hands-on activity to seal the deal, complete an assessment, extend the activity, and reevaluate the students' status.

the classroom by giving meaningful assignments to complete outside of the four walls of your class. You should review and follow up with your students periodically. As you build throughout the year, you want to reinforce what was already taught. This will make certain that there are no holes, cracks, or gaps in your foundation. Some of these activities can be posted in the students' folders or notebooks.

In addition to your daily or weekly plans, you want to make sure that you are prepared for anything. This is why it is best to plan ahead. If for some reason you cannot come to work, you need to have some type of emergency lesson plan available for the substitute or assistant. The next chapter will discuss emergency plans in more detail.

## KNOW IT FOR YOURSELF

When you wanted to pitch an idea in the corporate environment, you did your research and prepared yourself for obstacles that might stand in your way. You presented the facts in a way that grabbed the attention of your audience, giving them something to think about even after the meeting was over. Most likely, you followed up to answer lingering questions.

As an educator, you follow that same format, just to a different audience. You cannot present material that you do not know yourself. Learn the ins and outs of what you are about to teach. If there are different views on the topic, present them, and use them to engage the students in discussion.

## CREATING TESTS

As previously stated, you want to know how and when to go to the next skill with your students. Assessments or tests are a good point of reference. Many school districts may allow different grade levels to come up with tests or may already have some tests in place to guarantee that all students are learning the same information.

Even if you do not have a prewritten test, you can go to a more seasoned educator or write questions according to the information you are teaching that line up with the state's standards of learning. When writ-

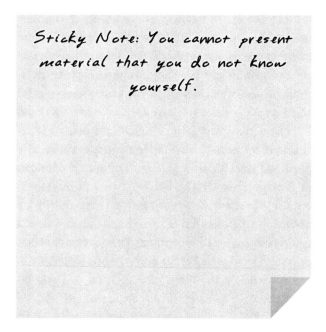

Sticky Note: You cannot present material that you do not know yourself.

ing these questions you need to keep your students in mind. You should tailor the language to fit what the students know and have been exposed to.

Assessments are a gateway to understanding what a student has comprehended and internalized. They should be well written and deal with the topic taught. Students should not be surprised about the questions

Sticky Note: Assessments are a gateway to understanding what a student has comprehended and internalized.

on a test. The test or assessment should be a review of the information already presented.

One school of thought is that an assessment should be created before planning the lesson. This way the lesson is planned around what the students are going to be tested on, and you do not risk testing them on something that was not taught. It also gives the educator direction in how to present the material.

## GRADE BOOK SETUP

Educators set up their grade books differently, so ask to look at a few. Other teachers or your mentor should be a good resource for this. You can also use the report card as a guide. Report cards list all of the subjects that students will need a grade for throughout the year.

In addition, many school districts provide software to their educators. Whether you are using software or paper and pencil, you want to make sure that you are keeping good academic records. Grades are recorded to show the academic progress of the student. You may need to use this information to show parents why their child got a certain grade or have information readily available for students who may transfer in the middle of the school year.

Software may also allow parents the opportunity to see how their child is performing. You should also be aware that some school districts collect grade books at the end of the year. This is very important if your lesson plans and grades are in one book. You may be required to turn in the whole book or tear out the grade sheets.

## REPORT CARDS/INTERIMS

If you have set up your grade book in accordance with the report card, adding grades should be a matter of plugging the correct grade into the slot. Of course, you

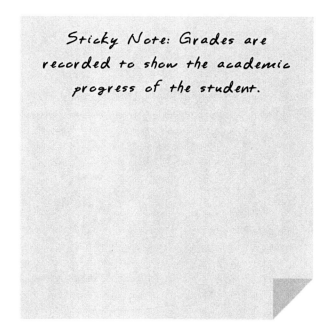

*Sticky Note: Grades are recorded to show the academic progress of the student.*

will have to average the grades that you have entered throughout the semester (giving more or less weight to some).

When adding comments you want to be tactful and honest. A good rule of thumb is to have one or two positive comments to go along with any negative challenges that a student may have. If the student does get a low grade in an area, address it in your comments. You do not want to get to a parent conference or reach the end of the year and have the parent be surprised because they never heard that their child's performance was below what was expected.

By being forthcoming with this information, you can give the parent and the student an opportunity to make adjustments to their current regimen. There are many comment lists available on the Internet as well as books available that you can use as a guide or base; you can then add your own twist or flair to the comment.

# 6

# Substitutes

Have you ever started a project and had to turn the project over at a crucial point? To make sure that the project proceeded successfully, you had to leave detailed instructions on the ins and outs, as well as identify all of the little quirks that your successor(s) might face. You thoroughly prepared them for any obstacles that they might face. You must have the same mindset whenever you are going to be away from the classroom.

**PREPARE YOUR STUDENTS**
None of us like surprises, so prepare your students. Let them know that you are going to be absent and how you expect them to conduct themselves while you are away. You do not have to give details of why you will be away, but remember, your students are accustomed to seeing your face and following your way of doing things. There are students who want and need structure and consistency. An unexpected absence could cause them to be uneasy and react negatively to another person filling in for you.

You should make sure that the person who is covering for you is capable of picking up where you left off. If you know that you will not be there, leave plans that are detailed and address all of the nuances that they may encounter. For example, if you have students who receive additional services, like speech or occupational therapy, write down the information and the times that these students are normally sent or picked up.

*Sticky Note: There are students who want and need structure and consistency; prepare these students for your time away.*

*Sticky Note: Leave plans that are detailed and address all of the nuances that they may encounter.*

*Sticky Note: Leave a detailed schedule of start and stop times for each activity, noting where there may be flexibility.*

Make certain that there are provisions within the plan for students who may complete their work early. The more that the substitute has to work with to keep the students on task, the better off things will be. A major part of managing a classroom is not having excessive periods of downtime. Give the substitute more than can be accomplished so that the students and the substitute are not left to their own devices.

Explain to the substitute that you are aware that all assignments may not be completed, but you wanted to make sure that she had more work than required, just in case some students completed their assignments early. All students should have some sort of list of things to do when they have completed their assignments. Stock that folder before you go and make the substitute aware that the folder is available.

The substitute will need to know your schedule because other teachers' schedules may be hinged to yours, like art, gym, or music. If the substitute is unaware of where the class should be, it can cause the students to miss valuable learning time in and out of your classroom. Leave a detailed schedule of start and stop times for each activity, noting where there may be flexibility.

The substitute will need to know when and where to send the attendance, what they should expect to collect (money, box tops, permission slips, etc.), and where it should be placed. The substitute will need the students' transportation chart, detailing who is picked up by a parent or guardian and who rides the bus, as well as their bus numbers (elementary).

In addition to your lesson plans and schedule, alert the substitute of issues that may arise due to behavior or personalities. Let them know who should not be grouped together or which students could be helpful should they need assistance, have questions, or need someone to run an errand.

A seating chart helps the substitute know who should be seated where and also helps to identify students. Identification of the students allows the substitute to know such details as who has allergies or a bladder control issue and must be released to the bathroom several times throughout the day. Also consider lunch if your students are in elementary school. The substitute will need to know where in the cafeteria your students are supposed to sit and if the student with allergies should sit at a table with other students or at a teacher-designated table.

## SAFETY DRILLS

Another issue to address is safety. You need to ensure that your substitute knows where to go in a fire drill,

*Sticky Note: A seating chart allows the substitute to pick out with ease students who could be helpful or who may have an issue that must be addressed.*

*Sticky Note: Keep a copy of your evacuation plan and lockdown procedures with your seating chart or attendance sheet.*

*Sticky Note: Something will come up that will cause you to need a backup plan.*

any other drill (tornado, hurricane, etc.), or real-life emergency or circumstance that may take place. Keep a copy of your evacuation plan and lockdown procedures with your seating chart or attendance sheet. Be mindful that these events can happen at any time. This information should be readily available even if someone is covering your classroom for as little as an hour.

## EMERGENCY PLANS

Inevitably, there will be a time when everything that is noted above will not be accomplished. Something will come up that will cause you to need a backup plan. In this case, you need to prepare emergency plans. These plans should be available in your classroom to be used in case of an emergency absence. Place them in an area where they can be easily located.

Emergency plans may contain material or activities that come from topics/concepts that have been taught in previous lessons. As you progress through the year, update these plans to ensure that the given work is current and relevant to the knowledge of the students. Another place to keep some of this work would be in individual folders or binders.

Plans should also include an up-to-date seating chart and a class schedule. You should have at least three days or more of activities that can be administered. Again, these activities should keep up with the rigor and relevancy of their current studies. The emergency plans are helpful when you are out for an extended period of time due to an unexpected illness or death of a loved one.

A substitute transition should be seamless, especially if your students have been following a routine. Students who have a consistent routine can function without someone feeding them their every move. Students should come in knowing where to turn in assignments, where to look to start any morning work, who goes where and when. The consistency of your routine will make the flow of the day easier for the substitute and the students.

To recap, a substitute packet should include a substitute information form, roster, seating chart, schedule, transportation chart, parent contact form, safety drill information, and regular or emergency lesson plans. Samples of forms needed in a substitute packet are located in appendix D.

# 7

# Assistants and Collaborations

It marks a big step in a man's development when he comes to realize that other men can be called in to help him do a better job than he can do alone.

—*Andrew Carnegie*

There are many school systems that are leaning more toward co-teaching. This is where two teachers collaborate on lessons in one or more subjects and present the subject to the class as a team. Many special education teachers are also co-teaching with general education teachers. In addition, many special education teachers work with an assistant who is mandated depending on the amount of students the teacher has assigned to them and the students' disabilities.

## RELATIONSHIP BUILDING

Sometimes working with an assistant or collaborating with a teacher can be more difficult than working with your students. You may have different views and opinions on what should be taught and how the information should be demonstrated or expressed. Although these difficulties exist, you have to remember why you are both there. It is not to show how smart you are individually, or demonstrate who can more effectively administer a lesson; you are there for one purpose: the students.

Just like in a marriage relationship, there should be some give and take. You never want your students to see the two of you at odds with one another. As you may know, students tend to use this knowledge to their advantage, so you should always show a unified

*Sticky Note: Relationships work when the parties involved decide to work hard and choose to look at the positive versus the negative.*

front. Relationships work when the parties involved decide to work hard and choose to look at the positive versus the negative.

## ASSISTANTS

Assistants can be a very valuable resource, especially when they have zeal or passion for the students and have been in the system for a while. Over a period of time these assistants have been privy to watching other teachers teach. They have seen what works and what does not work.

As a new teacher you must use this knowledge to your advantage. This knowledge may be helpful in

*Sticky Note: Assistants are more than people who can help you file, cut out templates, or deal with unruly students.*

building your relationship with your assistants. They are more than people who can help you file, cut out templates, or deal with unruly students. Assistants have great ideas, opinions, and suggestions that are not only important but valuable.

You must put on your listening ears and hear what your assistant has to say. Many companies progress and succeed on the ideas and collaboration of many and not just one. The president of an organization depends on many different departments and divisions for feedback. That feedback is used to propel an organization to new levels of growth and accomplishment.

An organization taps into its resources, the associates that they employ. You must figure out how your assistant best helps the efficiency and success of your classroom.

As with most things, there are issues that you should consider. You must ensure that your assistant understands whose classroom it is and you must clearly communicate your expectations. Unclear expectations could lead to unnecessary headaches and grief.

As in the corporate world, there may be freedom to a point, but you must stay within the goals and the objectives of the organization. Your assistant needs to stay within the goals and objectives that you have set for the classroom. Normally, when you meet your new class, you will present them with rules to abide by and you must do the same with your assistant.

On your first workday together you should have a heart to heart clearly defining how you would like things to run, when you are there and when you are away. These expectations should be revisited throughout the year to ensure that you stay in sync with one another the entire school year.

Take charge. You are your assistant's supervisor. This is important because when assistants have prior knowledge of how a topic is taught they may be tempted to wait until you are away and use that time to implement things that they feel would work better. Some of the things they initiate may be good, but some can undermine everything that you have established with your students. Before leaving make sure that you have detailed instructions and have asked if the assistant has suggestions, but once the plans are finalized, insist that they stick to the plans.

Leave nothing to the imagination. If you have plans that require something to be made or put together, leave a list of what and how many of the items should be used, if possible. That way, you will not return to

*Sticky Note: On your first workday together you should have a heart to heart clearly defining how you would like things to run, when you are there and when you are away.*

find supplies allotted for an upcoming project used while you were away.

*On the Front Lines:*

I had an assistant that changed my lesson every time I was absent. She would use materials and resources that I had not allotted. It was very frustrating, especially since I purchased most of my supplies myself. She had been in the school system a long time and was set in her ways or the way she saw a topic taught in the past.

She had a wealth of knowledge, but I felt like she undermined everything that I tried to establish with my students. I finally had to sit her down and tell her that I understand that it can be taught differently, but the way I write it in the lesson plans is the way I want it taught.

Christian

Although assistants may be mandated for your classroom, there are times that they may be pulled. If your school cannot find a substitute for another classroom, they will ask to use your assistant. Depending on your group this could be something that you could live with or something that bothers you.

You may also come into a situation where the assistant has been assigned other duties in the past and

*Sticky Note: Although assistants may be mandated for your classroom, there are times that they may be pulled.*

assumes those same duties when you arrive. If this is the case and it disrupts the flow of your classroom, speak to your principal about alternatives. The administration understands that you are new and you need those resources, and since this person is mandated to be in your classroom, they should be able to find a solution.

## COLLABORATION

In addition to working with an assistant, you may be required to collaborate with another teacher. Collaboration does not mean that you or the other teacher gains an assistant; it's quite the contrary. According to the Merriam-Webster Dictionary, a collaboration is "to work jointly with others or together especially in an intellectual endeavor." In other words, it is the putting together of minds to produce a lesson that will have a lasting impact on your students' academic success.

You should play on each other's strengths. If one has great artistic ability and the other has great presentation skills, plan a lesson where you both can complement one another. Remember that a president or lieutenant does not run an organization alone. There are many different aspects of the organization that are pulled together to complete the vision.

You must put your students first. If any disagreements arise settle them quickly and always look like a team when you are before your students. If you were competing for a new client and during the presentation your teammates contradicted one another and put down each other's ideas, you would more than likely lose the new client. In addition, you could possibly gain a bad reputation.

As a team, discuss the best way to engage your students in the learning process. Brainstorm and suggest many ideas, and be prepared to defend why you feel it may work. You can use a prior experience to demonstrate why your idea may be successful.

You should then narrow down your choices by choosing what may be more beneficial to your students. Depending on how your class is set up, you may be able to try a few different methods. Implement only what you agree will work, and if you find that your idea did not go over well, swallow your pride and try a new approach.

Remember that helping students through school is a team effort. Stay focused on the goal at hand and do not let personality quirks get in the way. Write a mission statement and keep it accessible. When you feel that things are starting to go awry, pull it out and remind yourself why you are there. Better yet, look around at your students and let their need to succeed motivate you to overcome the difficulties of working with someone else.

# 8

# Communication

For any project, business, or relationship to be successful, you must communicate. Communication is a transfer of information and ideas from one individual to another. Communication is the key to having a successful school year. You will need to stay in constant communication with the students, their parents, administration, and other staff members.

In a corporate environment, telephone and email conversations are the predominant forms of communication. These forms of communication allow you to keep in touch with your coworkers and clients. It also gives you an opportunity to keep track of what you have done. You can track the "what," "why," "when," "how," and "who" for every conversation.

*Sticky Note: Communication is the key to having a successful school year.*

The school environment is not much different. In addition to telephone and email, you will stay in contact by notes and flyers. These modes of communication can notify parents of upcoming events, meetings, or fundraising opportunities. In either situation, you want to make sure that you keep a record of all of your interaction with everyone you communicate with.

## PARENT COMMUNICATION

At the beginning, and throughout the school year, you should be in constant contact with the parents of the students you serve. Your first form of communication will most likely start with a letter introducing yourself to the parents. This back-to-school letter will give parents background information about you, as well as express your expectations for the upcoming year.

This letter could include attachments such as the supply list, class rules, policies to note, and an overview of what the students will be learning throughout the school year. A sample of a back-to-school letter is located in appendix B.

Field trip and event notification will be another reason for you to have to contact the parents. These forms should include what, where, when, why (what learning standards will apply), and how much. In addition, if you need chaperones, you will need a place for them to sign up. Of course, this form should include a section that they return and a section that they keep.

Sometimes it is necessary to request a meeting with the parents. If it is an Individual Education Plan (IEPs are discussed in chapter 10, "Special Education") meeting, you should have a meeting notice available in the software that your school division uses. This letter should give a brief synopsis of why you would like to see the parent, days and times that you are available, and your contact information.

You should periodically contact a parent with a good report on the child. Parents want to know that you are concerned, but they also want to know that their son or daughter displays qualities that deserve recognition and praise. It is not always easy to find something good to say about every child, but the child is bound to exhibit a behavior or demonstrate comprehension of a topic that you can contact the parent about. This can be communicated by a note or phone call.

Many schools use some sort of agenda. This is also a good place to write a quick note and receive quick notes from the parent. Let them know that the expectation is that they are checking it every day and that you will do so as well.

There are occasions where a note home will not be the best form of communication. There are students who lose or throw away any notes sent to a parent, especially if they know they have done something that is noteworthy. At the beginning of the year, make sure that you get updated information regarding the parent's or guardian's telephone, email, and home address.

You will need to ask for updated information periodically throughout the year. When using any of these modes of communication, stay professional, state who you are and the reason for the contact. Be aware that especially for students with IEPs these communications can be used in a court of law. You may want to adopt a policy of not using the child's name in email communication. For example, "Today during recess your son . . ."

*On the Front Lines:*

Parents are looking for you to be the expert. You may not always be able to tell them what they want to hear, but they need to hear it. They also need to hear the good. When you have to discuss challenges that the student is having, ensure that you have sufficient and undeniable backup, such as assessments and notes, to support what you have to tell them. I have good relationships with parents because I am sensitive, open, and honest.

I believe that sensitivity is the key. You should not only come to them with the issues but have a few suggestions of how to rectify the problem. No parent wants to hear that their child is having difficulties or is being difficult. Parents are most likely aware of any potential behaviors or academic challenges.

Some may be sensitive to this fact and feel like the world is against their child. I try to assure them that I want to give their child every opportunity to be successful and that I support them in their efforts. I want them to feel that we are a team and that we can get through anything if we work together.

Christian

Some schools allow you to set up a website to keep parents as well as students informed. If you have an opportunity to use this mode of communication, post as much information as you can here. Post your assignments for your classroom, upcoming school-wide events, special projects, homework, spelling lists, newsletters, and links to websites that may be helpful to parents and students throughout the year. Make sure that this is not a substitute for the other modes of communication, but use it as a tool to enhance your communication.

## STUDENT COMMUNICATION

Communicating with your students is something that you will do on a daily basis. You'll want to start the year off on the right foot. Just like you introduce yourself to the parents, introduce yourself to the students. You can do this with a simple postcard. This postcard can welcome them to your class or the school and let them know that you are looking forward to meeting and teaching them. This simple gesture can cause your students to be excited about the upcoming year, especially those in elementary school grades.

Once your students are in the classroom, you want to communicate your expectations, rules, and policies with them. You cannot assume that because the parents were made aware, the students will be aware. You

*Sticky Note: You should also have a designated area within the classroom for announcements and other areas of interest.*

should also have a designated area within the classroom for announcements and other areas of interest. In addition, if you are doing an activity that is out of your normal routine, make them aware of the changes in advance. This could be conveyed with a verbal announcement.

There are some students who thrive because of receiving praise or acknowledgment of a job well done.

*Sticky Note: Nonverbal and verbal cues can give the student the motivation necessary to strive to achieve or continue an acceptable behavior.*

There are many ways that you can communicate your appreciation for their effort and hard work. Nonverbal and verbal cues can give the student the motivation necessary to strive to achieve or continue an acceptable behavior.

A pat on the back, a thumbs up, a smile, or a simple "good job" could be more than sufficient. In other cases, the students may need more acknowledgment, like a sticker, certificate of achievement, or some agreed-on reward.

There are instances where a contingency contract stating a desired goal and/or behavior is in order. This contingency contract is an agreement between yourself and the student. It could be used for work that should be completed or to change a behavior that is being demonstrated. It should state the consequences for not achieving the desired goal, as well as reinforcements for achieving them. A sample contingency contract can be found in appendix E.

## ADMINISTRATION AND STAFF COMMUNICATION

In the corporate environment, you probably used email to initiate and respond to requests and business agendas. Email is a great way to track what you have done, what you have missed, and what you may need to do. In short, it is a great way to cover all of your bases; it leaves a trail.

There will be days that you are inundated with requests from the administration and staff as well as days where you will make several requests. Email is a great way to track what you have and have not responded to, as well as who has and has not responded to you. If there is ever an issue, you can use your email as a way of figuring out where the ball was dropped.

You may find that your principal is very busy. She is constantly being pulled in many directions at once. If you stop her in the hall to ask a question or to get clarity on something, be mindful that several others may have done the same. By the time three or four people stop her, she may not readily remember the conversation that she had with you.

To keep your issue at the forefront, send an email recapping your discussion. This may also be helpful when discussing issues with the staff, counselors, or therapist. This will ensure that the understanding you received from the discussion is the same understanding that the other parties have received.

*On the Front Lines:*

Coming from a corporate environment, it was drilled into me to cover myself. The best way to do that was to have an email trail. I was very surprised to find that some teachers did not even know their email address and never checked it.

Once I sent an email to a principal and never received a response. When I asked about it, the response was "I am professional. You know that I took care of it!" I did not know that it was taken care of. I was amazed that the mindset was so different.

It is a tool, in my opinion, that should be utilized by all. I have some parents who preferred the daily email update. They have expressed that they may not receive a note or know what homework was assigned. I would send them a short email about the events of the day before they left work and any homework in their child's agenda.

Christian

## COMMUNICATION DURING INSTRUCTION

You may find any form of communication during the school day is difficult, due to students depending on you to give instruction in the classroom. Sometimes planning periods and lunch are not enough time to contact everyone. Phone conversations with other staff members, administration, and parents should be kept short and to the point. Most likely you will not use this

Sticky Note: You may have an opportunity to "pop in" on a teacher, but before you come into a classroom make sure it is necessary.

method unless you are asking a quick question or need help and cannot leave your classroom.

You may have an opportunity to "pop in" on a teacher, but before you come into a classroom make sure it is necessary. Sometimes these kinds of interruptions can cause havoc in a classroom. The teacher will lose momentum, and the students will lose focus. If you must come in while a teacher is giving instruction, be mindful of how much time you spend in their classroom. Some teachers are very kind about these distractions, but a distraction is a distraction.

If you have an issue that does not need immediate attention, add it to your "to do" or reminder list. You may be able to ask these questions during a faculty meeting or before or after school.

# 9

# Students

The students you teach will change your life. They will make a permanent imprint on your life, some good and some bad. You will have students challenge the way you think, teach, and view the world. You may think that you are there for them, but in many ways you will find that you need each other to be successful.

Your students are coming from a variety of backgrounds. They will have a wide range of needs and concerns that may be a distraction or hindrance to their ability to learn. Their exposure to different cultures, mindsets, life experiences, morals, and values will unquestionably have an impact on how they approach education.

> Sticky Note: Their exposure to different cultures, mindsets, life experiences, morals, and values will unquestionably have an impact on how they approach education.

There will be students who have a great support system, where the parents are actively involved. These students will have parents or guardians enthusiastically advocating for them. They have access to resources and programs which can potentially cause them to be ahead of their classmates. They may have someone at home that they can go to when school, educationally and socially, becomes challenging for them. This support system will encourage them to read more, be more, and do more.

Unfortunately, the support system—or lack thereof—for other students is lacking guidance, money, and time. Students, when missing this support system, are not receiving what they need and deserve. Some students do not have someone they can go to at home or in their communities. The parents may have to work one or more jobs to supply basic necessities.

These parents might not see their child enough to read to them, check homework, or have time to come to the school and advocate for their child. They may not have funds to allocate resources and programs that will increase their child's ability to learn and grow.

There are several one- and two-family homes that cannot provide even the basic necessities, and these students have to deal with the reality of their lives outside of school, while trying to get an education. If you are not getting warm meals, have no bed to sleep in or no home to go to, education will not be a priority for you. You will be focused on survival. As an educator, these issues and circumstances must be at the forefront of your mind. It is the role of the teacher to become

*Sticky Note: Having a vested interest in your students' education is a nice place to start, but an even better place to start would be for you to sincerely invest in their lives.*

making them feel good should not be the totality of your approach.

Growth is not always about feeling good; there are growing pains that may occur. Some students will have to follow the rules set for your classroom when they do not have rules at home. Some students may not like the topic and that is okay, but they are all there to learn. Educators are required and have a responsibility to teach the standards set by the state.

The point of having a vested interest in your students' lives is to teach them in a way that they can relate to the material. There are different learning types that you must also be aware of. For the most part, students will either be visual, auditory, and/or kinesthetic learners. Having a vested interest in your students affords you the opportunity to observe their preferred method of learning.

The visual learner's strength is to learn by what they see. They will watch your facial expression and body language to help get an understanding. They will benefit from graphic organizers, illustrations, and pictures in textbooks. They will also be stimulated by visual displays, videos, overhead presentations, and handouts.

The auditory learner's strength is to learn by what they hear. Some topics may not become clear to them

an advocate for these students. You must overcome these challenges and give all of your students the best education possible.

It is very important to your success and, more importantly, the success of your students, to take a vested interest in their education. Having a vested interest in your students' education is a nice place to start, but an even better place to start would be for you to sincerely invest in their lives. You may be the only positive role model that some of these students see on a daily basis.

You have the power and the influence to make a difference in the life of a child. Your interest in them can cause them to read more, be more, and do more. You have an audience of students waiting for you to open up the world to them. You do not want to be in a classroom with that kind of major influence when all you want to do is collect a paycheck.

Get to know your students, their likes, dislikes, and dreams. Use what you have learned about them and apply it to how you teach the course of study. We all pay attention more when it is something that we want to hear or have an interest in. Does this mean that you have to do only the things that they like? Absolutely not! Appealing to them emotionally and

*Sticky Note: Growth is not always about feeling good; there are growing pains that may occur.*

Sticky Note: For the most part, students will either be visual, auditory, and/or kinesthetic learners.

Sticky Note: Do not provide a cookie cutter experience to your students; cater your lessons to the individuals.

until they have heard it out loud. When you model or talk through a problem, you are helping this type of learner. They will also benefit from group discussions, listening centers, and your verbal presentation.

The kinesthetic or tactile learner's strength is to learn by doing. They acquire knowledge from hands-on activities. They benefit from touching and movement. You will see a lot of movement in elementary classrooms, where students move to music or chants.

Once you have figured out how your students learn best, you can apply this information when you are planning a lesson. You can do a mixture of activities to differentiate your instruction and to capture your students' interest. Differentiation allows you to assess your students' level of readiness and plan for their success.

At this point, you have learned about your students' backgrounds, their exposure or life lessons, and how they best process information. Now you will take that information and meet each student where he or she is academically. You can do that by going into your classroom to teach individuals and not just provide a "cookie cutter" experience.

There are many strategies out there for developing a differentiated classroom. First, you may want to pay

attention to the material being taught. Are there students who have a working knowledge of this information? Are there others who have never been introduced to the concept? You may want to group your students, or present the material in a way that will engage students at different levels, having different activities available to accommodate a range of learners.

Sticky Note: Have different activities available to accommodate a range of learners.

You may also want to give students an opportunity to explore the concepts that you teach. Give them an opportunity to dream and figure out nuances of the topic. The students can complete assignments, individually, paired, or in small groups where they can discuss different outcomes.

Through the use of activities and manipulatives, students can identify many different ways to come to the same conclusion or discover what methods fail. In addition, give your students choices, varying the difficulty of the assignment depending on the students' level of readiness.

You will find that once you have captured your students' attention, your classroom management process will become much easier. Students who are engaged have less time to think about what they can do to get attention. Their attention is focused on the engaging activity that is presented before them.

Differentiation is a great approach to capturing those students who would normally fall through the cracks. Although this approach is great, it takes much thought and planning and does not happen overnight. It may be something that you have to implement in steps. You want to be an effective educator, and trying to do everything at once may not be realistic. Add new ways to differentiate as you master different parts of the process.

## CLASSROOM MANAGEMENT

Classroom management is of major importance. You need to be in an environment where you can teach, and your students need to be in an environment that is conducive to their learning. They need to feel safe and secure. They need to know that their basic needs are being met. You cannot move your class in the right direction without this key element in place.

Classroom management is made up of a variety of elements. Establishing a tone, expectations and consequences, as well as empowering your students are basic essentials that were all discussed in detail throughout chapter 4. In addition, chapter 5 talks about the importance of being prepared and organized to maintain order for yourself and your students. Seating and proximity to your students are also very helpful when managing your class.

*On the Front Lines:*

The first thing that popped in my head when I heard the words *classroom management* was *behavioral problems*. Although that is a part of it, behavior is not all that it encompasses. You can alleviate many behaviors just by being organized and prepared for your day. If you make sure that you involve your students and not just lecture them, they are more apt to participate than act out.

Christian

Behavior is one area that we will briefly discuss in this chapter. There are many individual, classroom, and whole-school initiatives out there. You will find that as students leave elementary school, methods change because the expectations are different. Listed below are just a few of the strategies used.

### Elementary

Traffic Light (Red, Yellow, and Green): Place clothespins on colored plates. Students all start on green and after a warning may be moved to yellow and/or red depending on the exhibited behavior. Students may have an opportunity to move back to a color if behavior improves.

Flip Cards in a Pocket Chart: Very similar to traffic light but color-coded cards are placed in a pocket chart and are flipped if behavior warrants.

Compliment Jars: If a student or the class receives a compliment anywhere in the school environment, an object is placed in a jar (cotton balls, beans, marbles, etc.). Once the jar is full, the students win a variety of prizes, which may include items like stickers, candy, toys, and cake.

Verbal Praise: Do not discount this very important tool. Giving a child words of praise, a pat on the back, or a thumbs up can go a long way.

Coupons: Coupons for homework passes; lunch with the teacher or principal; or extra computer, recess, or free time can be presented to students. These coupons can cover a variety of things and can be given individually or as a group.

Token Economy: Students can earn "money" and have an opportunity to spend it in the class or school store. This is also a great opportunity to teach basic math skills.

Warm and Fuzzy and Prickly: When a student says something nice to another student or does something nice for another student without being asked, the class is rewarded with a warm and fuzzy (cotton ball). If someone exhibits inappropriate behavior toward someone else, the class receives a prickly (toothpick). If the class receives more warm and fuzzies than pricklies after a predetermined amount of time, the class gets a party.

Parties: Students can work toward parties in various ways. Parties can be earned when everyone exhibits appropriate behavior, when everyone passes a test, when everyone brings in homework, and so forth. The party could be as simple as eating in the classroom with music playing, having pizza, or having cake and ice cream.

Certificates: Do not wait until an assembly to recognize an achievement or major improvement; do it in the moment, in front of the class.

Phone Calls or Notes Home: Parents and students appreciate phone calls recognizing special achievements.

Silent Lunch: Students must sit in a designated area and not talk during lunch.

### Middle and High School

You may see some of the items listed above in these settings as well as some additional strategies.

Cool-Off Zone: Students are allowed to go to a designated place to cool off and get themselves together before returning to class. This place is manned by teachers.

Referrals: Students' behavior is documented and sent to the office.

Detention: Students have to spend additional time at school.

Cleaning: Students are required to help clean a portion of the school.

Snacks: Students are not allowed to buy snacks from the cafeteria.

After-School Activities Revoked: Students cannot participate in sports or go to games, pep rallies, and dances.

Other very important elements of classroom management were discussed in this chapter: know your students, differentiate your instruction, and provide incentives. When all of these elements are applied, you will have a well-managed classroom. There are some unexpected situations that will present themselves, but with this combination of strategies your classroom issues should be few and far between.

*On the Front Lines:*
No one prepared me for the amount of time I would spend *every* day in classroom management. I only saw groups of students twice a month, so I had to reinforce discipline and review rules every day . . . from the first day of school to the last day. It never stopped, and for some classes behavior never got better.

Underwood

# Special Education

"Thrown under the bus," "a stepchild," and "a third wheel" are just a few ways that special education teachers describe their feelings about their treatment in the education field. This route into education may be one of the easiest because of the critical need for this type of teacher. Easy or not, it is something that you should consider long and hard.

You must understand the treatment you may receive may be more challenging than some of the students. If you decide that special education is the best fit for you, here are some things you should know.

## BOOKS

Books are hard to come by. You may find that there are many excuses for why you do not have your own set of books, or you may get the runaround from departments saying that your books were not part of "their" budget. Sometimes you may be sent to professional development opportunities and find a great product that will be instrumental in helping your students only to be disappointed because you cannot get the materials. The lack of books/materials nullifies the training because you cannot implement the program without them.

If you are able to get a full set of books, especially books that meet your students' needs, consider yourself lucky. Another thing to consider is that even if you get books for your students, you may not receive the teacher editions for yourself.

It is also very hard to order books because your students' readiness levels may vary greatly. You may have

students who barely know their alphabet and others who can read you under the table.

## SUPPLIES

Warning: Although parents send in supplies from the school's supply list, you may not receive any of them. Those supplies will go to the homeroom teachers of your students unless you are in a self-contained classroom. Depending on your location, it may not be feasible to ask the same parents for supplies for your room as well. In the current economy, most of your parents will simply not be able to afford the extra expense. This

*Sticky Note: Warning: Although parents send in supplies from the school's supply list, you may not receive any of them.*

means that you are responsible for tissues, sanitizers, markers, paper, and so forth.

Ask the teachers that you collaborate with if they are willing to share the supplies that they receive. You may find that some of them have stockpiled certain items over the years.

In some instances, you may be given a small budget to purchase a few things. If so, use it, and do not lose it. Budgets are tight and evolve over the year. Monies that were once allocated for one cause may dissipate or be reallocated to a new cause. When you place your order, think about items that you will need all year long (paper, notebooks, construction paper, glue, paint, etc.), and buy those things. There will most likely be several teachers ordering at the same time, so stay on top of your order and keep a copy of the purchase order.

*On the Front Lines:*

In my first year as a special education teacher, I spent well over $2000. I needed everything. I was always going to bookstores, teacher stores, and local stores to buy what I needed to implement a lesson. I could not believe how much money I was spending, but I felt like I could not go without the supplies. How was I going to offer the students quality differentiated instruction without supplies?

Christian

## CLASSROOM

There is a possibility that you will not have a classroom at all. You could be stuck anywhere, with a general education teacher, or you may be required to roam from place to place. It will mostly depend on the space available at your school. If you get a classroom it could be poorly furnished, have no windows, or be something that resembles a closet. The good news is that this is not always the case. There are rooms that are clean with matching furnishings.

## ASSISTANTS

If you get an assistant who is helpful, follows your vision for the class, and is willing to give you a hand with

*Sticky Note: Though your assistant's opinions may be strong, you still have to do what you feel is best for your students; ultimately, the responsibility for your students' achievement and success rests on your shoulders.*

the big and small jobs, count your blessings. Your assistant may have been in education for some time and may have strong opinions on how a classroom should be run, as well as how concepts should be taught.

Though your assistant's opinions may be strong, you still have to do what you feel is best for your students; ultimately, the responsibility for your students' achievement and success rests on your shoulders. You are the captain of your classroom, and there is more than one way to teach a lesson. At the same time, your assistant may be a valuable resource; do not discount what she has to offer. Listen to her ideas and suggestions and make an informed decision.

## PAPERWORK

You are required to maintain a nearly surmountable amount of paperwork. The most important document that you will maintain and live by is the Individual Education Plan (IEP). This document has been developed for each of your special education students to ensure that they receive an appropriate public education in the least restrictive environment. The plan will list the student's present level of performance, goals, accommodations/modifications, all services that the student is receiving, and other pertinent information regarding the student. This is a legally binding document that should be followed to the letter.

This document may require you to collect data about your students, tracking their progress. This data could be as simple as saving samples of their work throughout the course of the year to having notebooks full of information concerning how they are responding to teaching strategies and methods in the classroom. You will also have to ensure that all staff members and related services working with the student are aware of any accommodations/modifications that should be implemented throughout the school building.

Making them aware of these accommodations and modifications does not mean that you have the right to give these colleagues other pertinent information about the student. Make sure you get a clear understanding as to what you are allowed to share. You must respect your student's right to confidentiality.

### STUDENT OBSERVATIONS

You may be required to observe students who are in the process of a child study. The child study process consists of a team of professionals that decides whether the student is eligible to receive special education ser-

vices. Your role in the child study process may be to observe the student in a classroom setting for thirty minutes or more. You would record the student's interactions with the teacher and other students, as well as her participation in the activities presented.

### MEETINGS

Both the IEP meeting and child study require you to spend time outside of your classroom. IEPs are reviewed once a year for every student on your caseload. Every three years, students are evaluated to make sure they still qualify for special education services. During these reviews, you may discuss new goals; update the present level of performance; discuss any accommodations that the student may or may not need; and hear and incorporate the parents' concerns as well as those of the general education teacher, principal, speech therapist, occupational therapist, and physical therapist. If a member of the IEP team has concerns that need to be addressed outside of these review times, an IEP meeting can be called as often as needed.

These meetings can be very time consuming and stressful depending on the severity of concern that any member of the team has for the student's current progress or services. You must make sure to keep your

Sticky Note: The child study process consists of a team of professionals that decides whether the student is eligible to receive special education services.

Sticky Note: An IEP is a fluid document and can be changed at any time.

integrity in tact by tracking the student's progress as well as exploring all of the avenues that are available. You should not make promises that you cannot keep. Ensure that your meetings stay on track and are professional.

Just like you would prepare for a meeting for potential clients, prepare for your meetings. You will need to learn the meeting process as quickly as possible because you may have to facilitate a meeting before you are ready. If at all possible, request that your mentor or another experienced special education teacher completes several dry runs with you before a meeting takes place. This will narrow the possibility of your not looking prepared while in front of parents and other staff members.

Protect yourself. No one will protect you as well as you will. Keep a log of all communication that you have with parents, teachers, mentors, and administration in reference to any of your students. No matter how insignificant you believe these communications are, keep a record. If you do not do so, you may be subject to the blame game.

A parent, most likely, understands that there are challenges with their child. These parents could be at a loss on how to handle the challenges. On the other end

*Sticky Note: Keep a log of all communication that you have with parents, teachers, mentors, and administration in reference to any of your students.*

*Sticky Note: If a parent feels like you care, they will be more willing to work with you and hear your concerns when they arise.*

of the spectrum, there are parents who will blow a minor obstacle out of proportion and not be realistic on how it should be fixed. In either case, the parents need to be encouraged and informed. They are their child's advocate, for good or for worse. An engaged parent could make your life easier or much harder. There may be times that you cannot suggest a particular remedy, but if the parents are informed they may be able to get the student what she needs.

Venture to find some good in all of the students on your caseload. Periodically, relay a good report to the parent. It shows them that you see their child for more than someone with a disability and that you care. If parents feels like you care, they will be more willing to work with you and hear your concerns when they arise. In addition, if you have personal experience of a similar case, share the experience. It may put them at ease.

## ADMINISTRATION

In many cases you are on your own. You, after all, are the stepchild. Your request may go unanswered if you are not persistent. Even if you are persistent, you may become a sounding board for excuse after excuse about why something cannot be done. You will have to endure this all while you are being told how important you are and how much you are appreciated.

This is not necessarily your administration team's fault. There are many things that may be out of their control or things they simply cannot say. They may not have the power to fix or answer your needs. Remember school is also a business. They are looking at the big picture and trying to make the best decision for the school as a whole.

## OTHER NOTES

Some general education teachers look at you as more than a special education teacher. They may have a student who is having difficulty with comprehension and/or exhibits challenging behaviors and may want you to diagnose the student. This is not your job. Although you may have seen similar cases, leave it up to the professionals. Explain to them that you are not a doctor and, therefore, you cannot accurately diagnose the student. You should direct them to refer the child to the child study team to see if an evaluation is needed.

*On the Front Lines:*

Teaching special education can be so overwhelming. It is difficult trying to juggle curriculums for three different grade levels, especially when no one is truly on grade level. The books that I have are not the books that I need. My paperwork states that I teach third through fifth grades, but my students really range from pre-kindergarten to second grade.

It is difficult trying to figure out what to teach with three different levels, but it gets even harder when you also have to conduct meetings and complete required assessments. The assessments are basically a one-on-one session with your students and are very time consuming. It is very disheartening when all you want to do is do your students justice by teaching them something.

Christian

There are definitely challenges to overcome when teaching special education: no books, no supplies, expectations of teaching students individualized goals while having students on varying levels at the same time, and teaching when your time is consumed by meetings.

If you believe that the task is impossible, remember there are teachers doing this year in and year out. Most of them will tell you that the challenges are tough, but worth it. It is worth it because without teachers like you, these amazing students would fall through the cracks. Your perseverance can have a great impact on a life.

# 11

# Other Things You Need to Know

If you have not gathered by now, teaching encompasses much more than just being in a classroom. You are required to do many things other than stand in front of a class, conveying a topic. This chapter will briefly discuss the tell-tale indicators of a successful educator, culture, extra ways to make income, and fundraising.

## INDICATORS FOR SUCCESS

After reading this book you know that there will be many difficult experiences, but there are people like you who are immovable and face them head on. Dwight Clinton said, "The person with the right attitude and aptitude is better than the person with the right skills. You can teach skills, but you can't teach attitude." If you go into this career with the right attitude, you will go far.

Corporations are looking for forward thinkers who are engaging, creative, and convincing. They want someone who can motivate others, is proficient in the subject matter, and is organized. This person has to have the ability to work with a diverse group of individuals, anticipate problems, and have solutions. This person was you.

Now you are entering a community of other diligent, selfless, highly qualified individuals who just want to make a difference in the lives of young people by providing them with the best education possible. If you have any questions about whether this is the right career move for you, ask yourself these questions:

1. Am I a life-long learner? You will need to be in order to keep up with the strategies and methodologies needed to help your students be successful.
2. Am I a problem solver? Your approach to this career and its nuances, your students, and colleagues may be challenging, but you must explore every potential solution until the problem is resolved.
3. Do you communicate well? No matter how difficult the situation, the lines of communication must remain open and you need to communicate promptly and effectively.
4. Do you mind working long hours? This is not a nine-to-five job. There are many hours beyond the contractual time required.

*On the Front Lines:*

*Here are the responses of a principal and assistant principal to further clarify the indicators of one who should be in a classroom:*

Communication is a key tell-tale sign that administrators look for. A teacher has the responsibility of bridging the gap between themselves and their students, so good communication skills are a must. It's difficult sometimes to relate to people, especially children, so that learning can happen in their minds, but excellent teachers are masters of this. Relating to students on the students' level, these teachers have developed many ways to reach their students, and communicate using terrific speaking skills, visual aids, and even their body language.

In order for a teacher to be great, they must be admirable. Administrators look for teachers who lead lives of high moral ground, and they set an example to their students because of it. Really though, admirable teachers are more credible than others. We as people are much more likely to listen to those we admire, because we wish to be like them. Models of who we would like to be someday, great teachers help show us the way.

These are key qualities that administrators seek in individuals who are interested in becoming teachers: Positive Reinforcement, Leadership, Commitment, Understanding, Compassion and Caring, Confidence, and Preparation.

Hall-Lane

Essential characteristic keys to teaching are an ability to disaggregate data throughout the day and make educated instructional decisions based on data analysis, an ability to display flexibility on a continuum, an ability to be present with strong interpersonal skills and work ethic, a firm knowledge base regarding the content to be taught, a flair for teaching (teaching out of the box, allowing for highly engaging activities), as well as an ability to infuse technology in lessons on a continuum.

Persons who should be in the classroom are considered life-long learners. They feel a need to learn and grow with their students. Persons who see themselves as problem solvers are intent on finding the best means of assisting children in the learning process—no matter how many times the content is taught and how many ways they must teach it.

Williams

## CULTURE

The culture of my company is people focused. We understand that our people are our competitive advantage. We believe a work–life balance is important to productive and happy employees.

—*Mrs. Boots Corporate Trainer*

It is always great to work in an environment where you support your colleagues and your colleagues support you. In many school districts, the focus is not necessarily on you but on the business of educating children. There are definitely pockets of teachers and administrators who really support one another. Is this the case in every school district across the country? Probably not. There are businesses that stand out for their culture, and the same is true for schools.

*On the Front Lines:*
The culture of Clinton Investigations is one that stresses flawless execution of the promises we make to our clients. Our employees know they are empowered to make independent decisions, as long as those decisions are prudent for the circumstances at the time, and are calculated to provide value to the client.

We encourage forward thinking, especially when it comes to improving our products and services. Our employees are always occupied with getting better. We research, study, and compare other companies. What we find that they do well, we try to incorporate into our model. We also study their mistakes, and make sure we don't repeat them.

Clinton Investigations, LLC

Your school should have the same goals. Your clients are the families you serve. You want to serve them with flawless execution. You should feel like you can improve your classroom by thinking forward and finding ways to improve the student experience.

Professional development is one of the tools that you can use to strive to change the culture. You may speak to your principal about offering a professional development that will change or enhance the culture of your school.

It does not matter where you work; there will be little nuances and quirks that will get under your skin. How you handle and receive these challenges is completely up to you. Perfection eludes us all. That being said, we need to be careful about what we add or bring into our working environment. As stated in chapter 1, the school's culture should be a place where you, as well as your students, can flourish and grow.

Some people say "come with the solution not the problem." You can be aware of a needed area of growth without being part of the reason that growth does not manifest itself. You need to decide to not be part of the group that sits around and complains about the newest implementation of a program. If there are challenges, professionally express them to the proper channels. Be part of the solution.

*On the Front Lines:*

Any career will have challenges, and teaching is not an exception. The key to finding happiness is to focus on the small joys. Some days we may need a magnifying glass to view our purpose as a noble one. I gain a perspective each day into the profound level of patience and determination required to guide children with love. My students teach me the most invaluable lesson of all, to embrace life with a smile.

Utley

## INCOME

If you are like some career switchers, you may have taken a pay cut to follow this dream. There are a few ways that you may be able to make up for the loss of income without going outside of the school system. For a few extra hours a week, you can teach a student who is homebound, tutor after hours, coach, or become a jail instructor.

Students can be homebound for many reasons. The school system provides this service to these students from a licensed teacher. The teacher can go to the student's home, meet in a public facility, or in the case of a jail instructor, go to the prison to teach for a few hours a week.

The work given to the student is normally prepared by the teacher who was servicing the student in the general education environment, though there are a few cases where you may have to plan lessons for the student you are servicing. One rule may be that the homebound instruction cannot be given on school grounds or during school hours.

These are not mandatory assignments but something you can volunteer to do. The homebound assignment can be as short as a few days or could possibly extend through the school year. The pay for a homebound teacher is a good supplement to your income and is normally added to your current check.

One word of caution: if you are already overwhelmed with your current workload, do not add to your frustration by taking on one of these assignments.

Make sure that you can give all of your students your best. It will not be beneficial to you or your students if you are stretched too thin.

If your school has sport programs or extracurricular activities that require coaches, assistants, and/or leaders, you may be able to apply for one of these positions. Again, this is a time-consuming endeavor and, although noble, may require more time than you have to give.

These activities must be planned for; there are meetings that you may have to attend, practices that you have to be part of, as well as the actual events. The commitment to these activities is great. Consider your current workload and the stipend (pay); you can then realistically decide whether this is something that you should take on.

After you have received your full licensure, you may be able to be a mentor. This mentor position will allow you to give a new teacher an opportunity to learn and glean from your experience. It cannot be said enough that for any of these extra sources of income, make sure that you can be fully dedicated to the process. Many new teachers leave the profession because they are overwhelmed with the teaching process alone. If you are adding additional responsibilities, your stress levels may be worse.

Your challenge as a mentor is to be ahead of the game, so that nothing takes the teacher that you are mentoring by surprise. You should want to make this experience an exceptional one so that the students of the new teacher are getting what they need to be successful while maintaining success within your own classroom.

Depending on your district and the budget, you may be able to tutor students after school. This is especially critical for those grades that are nearing the standardized testing period. You may spend an extra hour or two in your classroom or somewhere in your building giving personalized instruction to students who have been identified as needing the extra resource.

## FUNDRAISING

One of the extra duties you may be accountable for is fundraising. The school needs money to run efficiently. You become a promoter for the school by getting the students in your classroom to participate in the many fundraisers that you will have throughout the year.

The fundraising campaign seems to be ongoing. You will constantly ask the students and their parents to buy into the different efforts that the school is promoting. Most of these efforts will benefit the school although not all of them. Some will benefit worthy organizations that have been in your community for years.

The fundraising may be as subtle as offering students a treat for a minimal fee a couple of times a week, or a bigger campaign where an outside source is used to sell products. It is your job to promote the big and small campaigns with excitement.

You are supposed to get the students excited about the prizes that they will receive individually or as a class. The Parent Teacher Association (PTA) may sponsor some of these events and give parties to classrooms that sell or bring in the most donated goods.

Most of these efforts will not directly affect your classroom, but may offset some of the expense of running a school. Depending on the location of your school, fundraising projects may or may not be stressed. Either way, remember the fundraisers are supposed to benefit the school and, ultimately, the students; do your part to make your school a success.

Support your PTA. The PTA events may have a direct effect on your classroom, especially if you have some sort of teacher grant program. Part of what the PTA does is raise money to help teachers get what they need in their classrooms. The PTA strives to help its teachers and the school, so if you can join your local PTA, join.

## YOU MADE THE RIGHT DECISION

Research states that over half of all new teachers quit within a five-year period. That statistic does not have to include you. This is not an easy career choice, but it is a great one. Now that you are going into this field more informed about what awaits you, you can go with the right attitude.

This attitude is one of success. Our young people need you to help shape them into our future leaders. There are challenges; it is hard work and can be very stressful, but it can and is done every day. Take this opportunity to leave the corporate environment and teach the next generation of business owners, doctors, and political figures.

# Appendix A

# Roster and Contact Forms

- Student Contact/Information Form
- Student Roster

## STUDENT CONTACT/INFORMATION FORM

| Student | Parent | Phone | Email | Birthday |
|---------|--------|-------|-------|----------|
|  |  |  |  |  |
|  |  |  |  |  |
|  |  |  |  |  |
|  |  |  |  |  |
|  |  |  |  |  |

## STUDENT ROSTER

| Name | Grade | Teacher Rcvd IEP Info | | | | | | Books Needed | Subjects to Be Taught by SPED | Notes |
|------|-------|------|------|------|------|------|------|------|------|------|
|      |       | P.E. | Art | Music | Library | Media | Guidance | ☐ Yes<br>☐ No; rec'd___ |      |      |
|      |       |      |      |      |      |      |      |      |      |      |
|      |       |      |      |      |      |      |      |      |      |      |
|      |       |      |      |      |      |      |      |      |      |      |
|      |       |      |      |      |      |      |      |      |      |      |
|      |       |      |      |      |      |      |      |      |      |      |
|      |       |      |      |      |      |      |      |      |      |      |
|      |       |      |      |      |      |      |      |      |      |      |
|      |       |      |      |      |      |      |      |      |      |      |
|      |       |      |      |      |      |      |      |      |      |      |
| **Resource:** |  |      |      |      |      |      |      |      |      |      |
|      |       |      |      |      |      |      |      |      |      |      |
|      |       |      |      |      |      |      |      |      |      |      |
|      |       |      |      |      |      |      |      |      |      |      |
|      |       |      |      |      |      |      |      |      |      |      |

# Appendix B

# Back-to-School Packet

- Back-to-School Agenda
- Back-to-School Teacher Letter
- Volunteer Forms
- Sample Classroom Schedule
- Information Update Form
- Daily Affirmations
- Insight Form
- Classroom Rules
- Teacher Introduction Letter
- Teacher Introduction Letter for Exceptional Education Students

**BACK-TO-SCHOOL AGENDA**

# Welcome
## to
## Back to School Night!

- A "Typical" Day in Kindergarten
  - Circle Time—*Calendar*, Classroom Helpers, Morning Message, Songs/Movement, Rhyme Time
  - Reading—Shared Reading, Literacy Activities, Star Students
  - Predictable Charts
  - Lunch
  - Recess
  - Specials
  - Unit—Science/Social Studies
  - Math—Sorting, Patterns, Numbers 0–10, Counting by 5s & 10s
  - Rest Time & Dismissal
- Reading—Name Wall, Morning Message, Predictable Charts & Books, Sight Words, Small Groups as Needed
- Procedures & Routines
  - Morning Routine: unpacking, stacking chairs, morning work/ centers
  - Quiet sign
  - Bathroom/ water fountain
  - Sitting on the carpet

## BACK-TO-SCHOOL TEACHER LETTER

Date

Dear Families,

Hello! My name is Your Teacher, and I am very happy to say that I will be your child's Kindergarten teacher for the 20xx–20xx school year! Kindergarten is an exciting year in which your child will grow socially, emotionally, and academically. It is a unique time in your child's educational experience in which we will learn many math skills and begin the adventure of reading. The children will also have many opportunities to explore their environment and develop motor skills through experiences including cooking, sensory activities, music, art, dramatic play, and hands-on activities in all areas of the curriculum.

I believe a Kindergarten classroom should be something like a "home away from home." As such, my aim is for our classroom to be a fun and caring place where the children feel comfortable and part of a community. We will learn to care about each other and work together. We welcome parent volunteers to participate in our wide variety of learning experiences. If you are interested in volunteering in our classroom, please fill out the form at the end of this letter and send it with your child to school.

This is my 4th year teaching Kindergarten, and I am excited to be part of Your Elementary School as we begin our second year! I grew up in Teacher County, and I graduated from College and the University of Virginia. I hold degrees in English and Creative Writing. As you can imagine, reading is one of my favorite subjects to teach! My first teaching experiences were with much older students—college students! I taught English and Creative Writing at a community college.

When I am not at school, I can be found reading, writing, watching movies, visiting friends, and traveling. I love to travel! I live in City Name and enjoy spending time with my family and my beagle. I also love to work with children outside of school, and I volunteer throughout the year at Camp, a camp held in Area Name for children with cancer. I have been involved with Camp for many years, and at least one weekend a month, I am up in the mountains attending a camp event. This experience is very rewarding, and it helps keep me grounded.

If you have any questions or concerns during the year, please feel free to contact me by phone or email. I will respond as soon as possible. Email is often the best way to reach me, if you have access to a computer. If you would like to meet with me in person, I am more than happy to make an appointment before or after school. Please see my contact information below.

In order to encourage community and sharing, all school supplies will be pooled together and distributed as needed. Students will not have their own individual supplies. This way, no child is ever without supplies.

Please take note of the forms included in your packet of information. These forms will alert us to your emergency contacts and transportation procedures. Also, if your child has any allergies or medical concerns that you would like me to know about, please feel free to discuss this with me. Please return these forms as soon as possible once you receive them!

Thank you for trusting me with your child. I am dedicated to providing the children with a caring and supportive environment where they can have fun learning and growing together. I look forward to your participation and input.

Let our Kindergarten adventure begin!

Sincerely,


Ms. Teacher

Contact Information:
Your Elementary School Phone: 555-555-5555
Email: yourname@yourdistrict.edu

**VOLUNTEER FORM**

# Calling All Volunteers!

If you are interested in volunteering in our classroom, please fill out the following information below. Thank you! ☺

Child's Name: _____

Name: _____

What is the best way to reach you? (You may list both if you wish!)

Phone: _____

Email: _____

Do you have any particular areas in which you'd like to volunteer?

_____ I can help wherever you need me!

_____ Special arts & crafts projects

_____ Cooking activities

_____ Class parties

Any ideas of your own? Please let me know! _____

**Please return this form with your child's daily folder!**

**VOLUNTEER FORM**

Dear Families,

If you are interested in volunteering in our classroom, please fill out the information below.

What is your preferred form of contact (phone, email, etc.)?
_____

Child's Name
_____

Your Name
_____

Please list or check any particular area in which you would like to volunteer.

_____ I can help whenever you need me!

_____ Special events and projects

_____ Cooking Activities

_____ Class Parties

_____ Guest Reader

_____ Chaperone on Field Trips

_____ Other _____

Thank you for supporting our class!

## SAMPLE CLASSROOM SCHEDULE

### Ms. Educator Classroom Schedule
### Kindergarten, Room 777
### 20xx–20xx

| | 8:25–9:10 | 9:10–10:45 | 10:55–11:25 | 11:30–12:00 | 12:00–12:45 | 12:45–1:30 | 1:30–1:45 | 1:45–2:30 | 2:30–3:00 | 3:05–3:20 |
|---|---|---|---|---|---|---|---|---|---|---|
| Monday | Morning Work/ Centers | Reading—Calendar, Building Blocks | Lunch | Reading: Predictable Charts | Recess: 12–12:20 Unit: 12:25–12:45 | Music | Snack | Math | Rest Time | Read Aloud/ Dismissal |
| Tuesday | Morning Work/ Centers | Reading—Calendar, Bldg. Blocks P.E.: 10–10:30 | Lunch | Reading: Pred. Charts | Recess | Unit | Snack | Math | Rest Time | Read Aloud/ Dismissal |
| Wednesday | Morning Work/ Centers | Reading—Calendar, Bldg. Blocks | Lunch | Reading: Pred. Charts | P.E.: 12–12:30 Recess: 12:30–1:00 | Unit: 1:00–1:30 | Snack | Math | Rest Time | Read Aloud/ Dismissal |
| Thursday | Morning Work/ Centers | Reading—Calendar, Bldg. Blocks Guidance: 10–10:30 | Lunch | Reading: Pred. Charts | Library: 12–12:30 Recess: 12:30–1:00 | Unit: 1:00–1:30 | Snack | Math | Rest Time | Read Aloud/ Dismissal |
| Friday | Morning Work/ Centers | Reading—Calendar, Bldg. Blocks | Lunch | Reading: Pred. Charts | Recess: 12–12:20 Unit: 12:25–12:45 | Art | Snack | Math | Rest Time | Read Aloud/ Dismissal |

**INFROMATION UPDATE FORM**

Dear Families,

During the year, I may need to contact you and I would like to ensure that I have the best and most up-to-date information. Please complete the form below.

What is your preferred form of contact (phone, email, etc.)?

_____

Name

_____

Address

_____

_____

_____

Home Phone

_____

Cell Phone

_____

Work Phone

_____

Email

_____

Best time to contact you

_____

Notes

_____

_____

_____

_____

_____

## DAILY AFFIRMATIONS

**To be spoken by teacher and student . . .**

I believe in myself.

I am smart.

I am ready to learn.

I am an explorer of learning.

My work is not too hard.

I can learn anything!

**Student must tell someone else . . .**

I believe in you.

You are smart.

You are ready to learn.

You are an explorer of learning.

Your work is not too hard.

You can learn anything!

**Parents**—You are welcome to do this activity with your child as **many times** as you wish.

**INSIGHT FORM**

When asked, especially the first few days of school, our children may not always respond the way we think they may. So I need your help . . . Tell me about your child.

Nickname
_____

Favorite Color
_____

Favorite Activity
_____

Favorite Toy/Game
_____

Favorite Food(s)
_____

Favorite Type of Clothing
_____

Favorite Sport
_____

Who do they look up to/want to be like?
_____

Favorite Television Show
_____

Favorite Video Game
_____

Any Other Favorites . . .
_____
_____
_____

Parents: How would you prefer I contact you? (Please list phone numbers and/or email addresses here.)
_____

Thank You!
Your Teacher

**CLASSROOM RULES**

## Respect Yourself and Others

## Follow Directions

## Always Do Your Best

Rewards
Verbal Praise
Hand Stamp
Phone Call Home
Note Home (Praise Note in attachments)
Lunch with Teacher
Student Choice
Whole Class Party
Whole Class Movie

Consequences
Warning/reminder of rule
Student Conference
Parent Call
Parent Note (Parent Note in attachment)
Parent Conference
Contingency Contract
Detention (Student Behavior Discipline Action
    Report)

**TEACHER INTRODUCTION LETTER**

**School Name**

Dear Parents,

Welcome to the **20xx–20xx** school year at Your Elementary School, where learning is an adventure (you can use your motto)! I am excited about meeting your little explorer. Over the next school year, we will be exploring the world of learning, while having fun and striving to meet our goals.

It is my mission to promote learning by nurturing and encouraging your child to be the best student that he/she can be. I will do that, in part, by affirming and focusing on your child's strengths, his/her way of learning, as well as providing an atmosphere where he/she can feel comfortable exploring new materials. It truly does take a village to raise a child, and I believe that we can have great success if we have open communication and work together as a team.

I am **Name** and I have a Masters Degree in Special Education and a Bachelor's Degree in Behavioral Science. Beyond my schooling, I can relate to you parent to parent. I have two sons who will be attending Your Elementary; one of my sons had challenges in learning the way that all of his peers did. Through the eyes of his very caring teachers, I watched my son go from a caterpillar to a butterfly. There are enough people out there who focus on the negative; I want to focus on your child's positive talents to help him/her reach his/her full potential.

I look forward to working with you and your child this year. If you have any questions/concerns that you would like to discuss with me, please feel free to contact me via email at youremail@districtserver.edu during school hours. If you would like to see me face to face, please email me to set up an appointment.

Sincerely,


Mrs. Name
Teacher
Your Elementary School

**TEACHER INTRODUCTION LETTER FOR EXCEPTIONAL EDUCATION STUDENTS**

Your HIGH SCHOOL
10700 Broad Street
Your Town, USA 55555

Office: (555) 555-5555
Fax: (555) 555-5555
email@yourdistrict.us

August 28, 20xx

Dear Parent or Guardian,

Let me be the first to welcome you to the 20xx–20xx school year at Your High School. My name is Your Teacher and I will be your child's case manager this year. I am very excited about working with you and your child. Throughout this year, I will make sure your child's IEP is followed and that the process is going in a positive direction. This task cannot be done by one person, so your help is needed to stop any obstacles before they arise. I feel that good communication is the key to a successful year, so I will be calling and sending things home to keep you informed.

You may contact me any time, either by phone ( ) or by email ( ). Thanks for your time, and I look forward to having a great year!

Sincerely,


Mrs. Your Teacher
Special Ed Teacher

# Appendix C

# Letters, Notes, and Field Trips

- A Note from the Teacher
- In Danger of Failing Letter
- Field Trip Form
- Parent-Teacher Conference Request Letter
- Explanation of Rules and Consequences Letter

**A NOTE FROM THE TEACHER**

To _____ Date _____

_____

_____

_____

_____

_____

From _____

**A NOTE FROM THE TEACHER**

To _____ Date _____

_____

_____

_____

_____

_____

From _____

**IN DANGER OF FAILING LETTER**

YOUR HIGH SCHOOL
7053 Messer Road
Richmond, VA 23231-5500

Office: (555) 555-5555
Fax: (555) 555-5555

February 1, 20xx

Dear Parent/Guardian:

I am Mrs. Good Teacher, your child's English 9 teacher at Your High School. We have just completed the second nine weeks and the first semester. I am writing because I am concerned that your child, _____, is in danger of failing for the year. Your child's lack of progress is due to one or more of the following reasons:

_____ Excessive absences
_____ Failure to complete class/homework assignments
_____ Failure to complete makeup work
_____ Failure to make up tests and/or quizzes
_____ Other _____

Your child can approach me at any time for a progress report and a list of missing assignments. If you need to get in contact with me, I can be reached at (555) 555–5555. Please leave a message with the telephone number and best time to contact you. You may also email me at yourteacher@district.us.

Please complete and return the bottom portion of this letter so I can confirm you are aware of your child's progress. This confirmation must be returned by Friday, February 5, 20xx. I hope that we can work out a plan of action together to ensure your child's success in English.

Sincerely,


Good Teacher
--------------------------------------------------------------------------------------------------------------------------
Parent's name: _____
Student's name: _____

Please sign below to indicate that you have received notification of your child's progress and check whether you would like to schedule a conference.

_____ Yes, I would like to schedule a conference.
_____ No, I do not wish a conference at this time.


_____        _____

Signature                                Phone number

**FIELD TRIP FORM**

Dear Parents:

Our class will be going on a field trip to the **Place of Field Trip** on **Field Trip Date**. We will leave at **Departure Time** and return at **Return Time**. This trip covers the following standard of learning **Covered Standard**. The purpose of this trip is to **State Purpose of Trip**.

The cost of this field trip is $**Cost of Trip** per person. This fee includes **Itemized Fee List**. We welcome you to meet us at the venue. Any admissions purchased at the ticket booth will be $**Cost at Event**.

This field trip is **non-refundable**. Your child will need to wear clothing that is suitable for **Suggested Clothing**.

It is recommended that your child bring **Suggested Additional Funds** to cover lunch and snacks.

Monies are due by **Date funds are Due**. Please sign and return the permission slip below.

Thank you.

---------------------------------------------------------------------------------------------------------------

My child, _____, has permission to attend the field trip to _____ on _____. The money for this trip is enclosed.
I, _____ would like to be a chaperone during this field trip. An additional $ _____ is enclosed.

_____

Parent/Guardian

## PARENT-TEACHER CONFERENCE REQUEST LETTER

Date

Teacher's Name
School Name
School Address
School City, State Zip

Dear **Parent's Name:**

I am requesting a parent conference with you in regard to **Student's Name.** **Student's Name** is having difficulty with **Area of Difficulty,** and I would like to discuss how we can work as a team to get him/her back on track.

I am available Monday–Friday from **Time–Time.** I would like to schedule this meeting for **Time** at **School Location.** Please let me know if you can attend or respond with a day and time that is more suitable for you.

Thank you in advance for your help in resolving this matter.

Sincerely,


**Teacher Name**

## EXPLANATION OF RULES AND CONSEQUENCES LETTER

September 20xx

Dear Parents,

We strive together to all be successful. To ensure success and safety of all students, we must have rules, consequences, and rewards in place. We take following the rules very seriously. Please remind your child of the importance of having and following rules.

As previously mentioned, a daily folder is sent home on a daily basis with a calendar for your child to record their daily behavior. The folder MUST be signed and returned on a daily basis. The behavior system in place is based on earning money (coins). The students will earn a particular value each day for staying on green. The value will increase as the year progresses. At first, we will start off earning pennies but we will move on to nickels, dimes, and quarters. The object of using the money system is to reinforce the students' ability to count a collection of coins and be able to exchange coins for an equal value (e.g., exchange five pennies for a nickel). Please review the rules, consequences, and rewards with your child. These rules are schoolwide! **Please sign and cut off the bottom portion of this paper (on the second page) by Friday, September 10th, 20xx.**

Thank you so much,

Teacher
teacher@ed.us

Rules:
1. Use Appropriate Voice Levels (1, 2, 3, and 4): 1 = NO Talking, 2 = Whisper, 3 = Talking in a Normal Tone/ Conversing with Your Neighbor, 4 = Outside/Loud.
2. Raise Your Hand AND Wait Your Turn to Speak
3. Use Your Walking Feet While Indoors
4. Stay in Your Assigned Area
5. Treat Everyone with Respect
6. Keep Your Hands, Feet, and ALL Objects to Yourself.
7. Always Tell the Truth
8. Always Try Your Best

Consequences:
1. *Green:* Great Day! I am so proud of your child! Your child followed all of the rules today!
2. *White:* Your child had their card changed once today and did not earn their coin(s) for today.
3. *Yellow:* Your child had their card changed two times today and had to return some of their coins (a certain value depending on the week—the value will increase as the year progresses and they earn more money).
4. *Red:* Your child had their card changed three times today! This is unacceptable and will not be tolerated! Your child lost ALL of his/her coins today and depending on the severity of frequency of occurrences, your child will receive an office referral, after-school detention, care center, or out of school suspension.

**Rewards:**
1. Treats
2. "Gotta Get Its"
3. Treasure Box Each Friday
4. Marbles/Marble Jar Parties
5. Reading Box Each Friday—Read five books *at home* each week

------------------------------------------------------------------------------------------------

My child _____ and I have reviewed and understand the importance of the rules, consequences, and rewards. My child will abide by them.

Signature _____

# Appendix D

# Substitute Packets and Lesson Plans

- Emergency Lesson Plans
- Seating Chart
- Substitute Teacher Information
- Detailed Lesson Plan Form
- Weekly Lesson Plan Form

**EMERGENCY LESSON PLANS**

**Day 1**

Most students will need instructions and reading material read to them. You can complete the reading portion of these activities as a group and let the students select or write their answer individually. If a student cannot spell a word, direct them to try first (with the exception of Student 1, Student 2, and Student 3).

*Social Studies*

Complete "Find Your Way around the Map" Worksheet.

*Language Arts*

After handing out the story below, ask the students if they think it is a fiction (fantasy) or non-fiction story. Why or why not? Ask what they think a dragon should be fed.

Echo Read "What to Feed a Dragon."

Complete associated worksheets (3).

If you have additional time, have the students draw a picture of them feeding a dragon its favorite treat.

In addition complete the "What does it mean?" sheet.

*Math*

Complete Place Value Sheet.

Complete Review: Applying Math Skills.

*Science*

Complete States of Matter sort.

**Day 2**

*Social Studies*

Complete "Know the States" Worksheet.

*Language Arts*

After handing out the story below, ask the students what they think will happen in the story. Give them a few moments to write their predictions down.

Echo Read "The Hidden Treasure."

Have students write down how the story was different from their predictions.

Complete associated worksheet.

In addition complete the "What Fact and Opinion" sheets.

*Math*

Complete Fairy Tale Subtraction.

Complete Number Sense Worksheet.

*Science*

Complete Paper Tower Activity. See Instruction sheet for directions.

Newspaper is behind the bookshelves near the lamp, back wall side.

Rulers are in the pink drawers located in the front of the classroom.

**Day 3**

*Social Studies*

Complete President's Day Writing–If I were president . . .

*Language Arts*

After handing out the story below, ask the students if anyone has heard of Dr. Seuss. Who is he?

Read "Dr. Seuss: Helping Kids Learn to Read."

Complete associated worksheet.

Read a Dr. Seuss book. Students can choose. His books are under Ms. Holmes's desk.

If you have additional time, have the students draw a picture of their favorite Dr. Seuss story.

In addition complete the "Real or Fantasy" sheet.

*Math*

Complete cake multiplication worksheets.

*Science*

Complete Penny Cup Game. See instruction sheet and follow directions.

Cups are near the microwave.

**SEATING CHART**

*Note:* At no time can Student 1 and Student 2 sit next to one another.

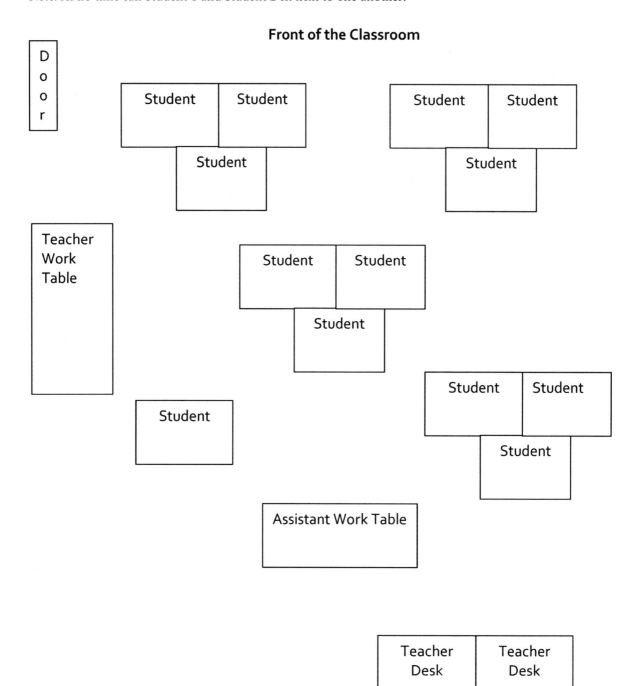

## Front of the Classroom

## SUBSTITUTE TEACHER INFORMATION

*Notes:* Student 1 and Student 2 are not allowed to participate in ANY activity together. They cannot go to any resource activities or class activities together, including lunch, bathroom breaks, and recess.

### Emergency Procedures

If there is a fire alarm, go out of the side double doors, across from door to room. Proceed straight to the gate. The students should face the gate with hands over mouths. You must bring the class roll with you as you leave the building and close the door to the classroom. The class schedule can be used as the class roll. The schedule is included in the packet and also hangs on the board near the filing cabinets.

### People to Contact

On the chalkboard there is a phone directory. It is yellow and in a plastic sleeve.

Teacher: Teacher of Room 100 knows the schedule and should be able to help with any situations that may arise. Teacher of Room 201 is the next classroom over if you have a quick general question.

Student Helpers: Student 4, Student 5, Student 6, and Student 7 are all dependable helpers.

Principal: Ms. Jones

Assistant Principal: Mr. Smith

### Classroom Procedures

The Attendance cards will either be in the mailbox labeled Teacher/Assistant (in the office) or on the kidney table in the classroom. If students are present just leave their cards inside of the envelope. If students are tardy put a "T" on the correct date on their card. If they are absent just put an "I". **Only write in pencil.** Thank you.

### Lunch

Students go to lunch at 12:15 and leave at 12:50. Most days they are given a fruit/vegetable snack that must be picked up by you. Just go to the register and tell them how many students and teachers are in the classroom.

### Bathroom

There are two scheduled bathroom breaks. They are 10 a.m. and on the way back from lunch. If at all possible students need to stick to this schedule. If they must go outside of these times, please ensure that they take nothing with them (markers, toys, etc.). When going as a group **no more than two boys** should go at a time.

***Student 4 and Student 8 are exceptions** to the above rule. Due to medical challenges they are allowed to go to the bathroom as many times as necessary.

### Recess

Recess is from 12:00–12:10. Student 1 and Student 2 are **NOT** allowed to play near each other. These students can be aggressive toward others and should be watched carefully even apart from one another.

### Dismissal

Dismissal normally begins between 2:35 and 2:40. The bus rider/parent pickup schedule is located on the front board in the right corner.

### Discipline

Students all have three rocks on their desks. These rocks are the equivalent to money. After a warning a rock should be taken. If the behavior continues, another rock should be taken, and so on. At the end of the day, please note anyone who has had a rock taken and they will lose "money" for that day.

The students also have a class disciple policy. Warm and Fuzzies (cotton balls) are given to the class when they are helpful to one another or you without being asked. Pricklies (toothpicks) are given when they are verbally and physically hurtful to a classmate or disruptive. Warm and Fuzzies can lead to a class party at the end of the month. Cotton balls and toothpicks are located on top of the filing cabinets behind the front door. They are to be put into the clear magnetic holder attached to the right corner of the whiteboard.

In addition, there are Behavioral Specialists who periodically sit in the classroom. If need be, they can take a student out or assist in diffusing a situation.

## DETAILED LESSON PLAN FORM

| Teacher: | | Date to Implement | |
|----------|--|-------------------|--|
| **Subject:** | | | |
| | | | |
| **State Standard:** | | | |
| | | | |
| **Objective:** | | | |
| | | | |
| **Materials Needed:** | | | |
| | | | |
| **Location of Materials:** | | | |
| | | | |
| **Website/Technology Used: (if applicable)** | | | |
| | | | |
| **How to Access Website:** | | | |
| | | | |
| **Student Information:** | | | |
| | | | |
| **How to Begin: (Before)** | | | |
| | | | |
| **Instruction/Modeling:** | | | |
| | | | |
| **Independent Activity:** | | | |
| | | | |
| **Closing:** | | | |
| | | | |
| **Assessment:** | | | |
| | | | |
| **Homework:** | | | |
| | | | |
| **Additional Notes:** | | | |
| | | | |

## WEEKLY LESSON PLAN FORM

|  | Monday | Tuesday | Wednesday | Thursday | Friday |
|---|---|---|---|---|---|
| Subject:<br><br>Standard:<br><br>Objective: |  |  |  |  |  |
| Before:<br><br>During:<br><br>After: |  |  |  |  |  |
| Subject:<br><br>Standard:<br><br>Objective: |  |  |  |  |  |
| Before:<br><br>During:<br><br>After: |  |  |  |  |  |

# Appendix E

# Calendars and Other Forms

- ABC Chart
- Behavior Cards
- Contingency Plan
- Frequency Chart
- Spelling Homework Sample
- IEP Draft Letter
- Lunch and Specials Schedule
- Math Homework Sample
- Monthly Newsletter Sample
- Observation Form
- Professional Goals and Objectives Sample
- Reading Book Bags
- Behavior Rock Log
- Student Behavior Rock Log
- Spelling Contract

**ABC CHART**

Student Name: _____ Date: _____

Description of Setting of Observation: _____

| Antecedent (event that triggered behavior) | Behavior (behavior exhibited) | Consequence (result) |
|---|---|---|
|  |  |  |
|  |  |  |
|  |  |  |

**BEHAVIOR CARDS**

Quiet

I will raise my hand to speak.

I will not skip or run.

I will WALK.

Sit Down

Hands to Yourself

I will not skip or run.

I will WALK.

Sit Down

Listen to Teacher

## CONTINGENCY PLAN

This is an agreement between **Student's Name** and **Teacher's Name**. This contract will begin on **Date** and ends on **Date.**

The contract will be reviewed on **Date** and **Date** to reevaluate and determine whether all parties are in compliance with the terms.

The review will also be an opportunity to make any necessary adjustments to this agreement.

The terms of the agreement are as follows:
  The student will **List student responsibility.**
  The teacher will **List teacher responsibilty.**

If the student fulfills his or her part of the contract, the student will receive the agreed-on reward from the teacher. However, if the student fails to fulfill his or her part of the contract, the reward will be withheld.

Student's Signature _____

Teacher's Signature _____

**FREQUENCY CHART**

Student Name: _____     Date Initiated: _____

Type of Behaviors Exhibited: 1. _____

                                2. _____

                                3. _____

| Date | | | | 1 | 2 | 3 | 4 | 5 | 6 | 7 | 8 | 9 | 10 | 11 | 12 | 13 | 14 | 15 | 16 | 17 | 18 | 19 | 20 | | Total |
|---|---|---|---|---|---|---|---|---|---|---|---|---|---|---|---|---|---|---|---|---|---|---|---|---|---|
| | | | | 1 | 2 | 3 | 4 | 5 | 6 | 7 | 8 | 9 | 10 | 11 | 12 | 13 | 14 | 15 | 16 | 17 | 18 | 19 | 20 | | |
| | | | | 1 | 2 | 3 | 4 | 5 | 6 | 7 | 8 | 9 | 10 | 11 | 12 | 13 | 14 | 15 | 16 | 17 | 18 | 19 | 20 | | |
| | | | | 1 | 2 | 3 | 4 | 5 | 6 | 7 | 8 | 9 | 10 | 11 | 12 | 13 | 14 | 15 | 16 | 17 | 18 | 19 | 20 | | |
| | | | | 1 | 2 | 3 | 4 | 5 | 6 | 7 | 8 | 9 | 10 | 11 | 12 | 13 | 14 | 15 | 16 | 17 | 18 | 19 | 20 | | |
| | | | | 1 | 2 | 3 | 4 | 5 | 6 | 7 | 8 | 9 | 10 | 11 | 12 | 13 | 14 | 15 | 16 | 17 | 18 | 19 | 20 | | |
| | | | | | | | | | | | | | | | | | | Total for the Week | | | | | | | |

| | | | | 1 | 2 | 3 | 4 | 5 | 6 | 7 | 8 | 9 | 10 | 11 | 12 | 13 | 14 | 15 | 16 | 17 | 18 | 19 | 20 | | |
|---|---|---|---|---|---|---|---|---|---|---|---|---|---|---|---|---|---|---|---|---|---|---|---|---|---|
| | | | | 1 | 2 | 3 | 4 | 5 | 6 | 7 | 8 | 9 | 10 | 11 | 12 | 13 | 14 | 15 | 16 | 17 | 18 | 19 | 20 | | |
| | | | | 1 | 2 | 3 | 4 | 5 | 6 | 7 | 8 | 9 | 10 | 11 | 12 | 13 | 14 | 15 | 16 | 17 | 18 | 19 | 20 | | |
| | | | | 1 | 2 | 3 | 4 | 5 | 6 | 7 | 8 | 9 | 10 | 11 | 12 | 13 | 14 | 15 | 16 | 17 | 18 | 19 | 20 | | |
| | | | | 1 | 2 | 3 | 4 | 5 | 6 | 7 | 8 | 9 | 10 | 11 | 12 | 13 | 14 | 15 | 16 | 17 | 18 | 19 | 20 | | |
| | | | | 1 | 2 | 3 | 4 | 5 | 6 | 7 | 8 | 9 | 10 | 11 | 12 | 13 | 14 | 15 | 16 | 17 | 18 | 19 | 20 | | |
| | | | | | | | | | | | | | | | | | | Total for the Week | | | | | | | |

| | | | | 1 | 2 | 3 | 4 | 5 | 6 | 7 | 8 | 9 | 10 | 11 | 12 | 13 | 14 | 15 | 16 | 17 | 18 | 19 | 20 | | |
|---|---|---|---|---|---|---|---|---|---|---|---|---|---|---|---|---|---|---|---|---|---|---|---|---|---|
| | | | | 1 | 2 | 3 | 4 | 5 | 6 | 7 | 8 | 9 | 10 | 11 | 12 | 13 | 14 | 15 | 16 | 17 | 18 | 19 | 20 | | |
| | | | | 1 | 2 | 3 | 4 | 5 | 6 | 7 | 8 | 9 | 10 | 11 | 12 | 13 | 14 | 15 | 16 | 17 | 18 | 19 | 20 | | |
| | | | | 1 | 2 | 3 | 4 | 5 | 6 | 7 | 8 | 9 | 10 | 11 | 12 | 13 | 14 | 15 | 16 | 17 | 18 | 19 | 20 | | |
| | | | | 1 | 2 | 3 | 4 | 5 | 6 | 7 | 8 | 9 | 10 | 11 | 12 | 13 | 14 | 15 | 16 | 17 | 18 | 19 | 20 | | |
| | | | | 1 | 2 | 3 | 4 | 5 | 6 | 7 | 8 | 9 | 10 | 11 | 12 | 13 | 14 | 15 | 16 | 17 | 18 | 19 | 20 | | |
| | | | | | | | | | | | | | | | | | | Total for the Week | | | | | | | |

Frequency of Behavior

Total for 3 Weeks ▨

**SPELLING HOMEWORK SAMPLE**

Name _____

Use your spelling words to complete four activities (one a day).
When you finish an activity, color the box.
Turn in all assignments on Friday.

| Triangle your words. example, flag | Draw a picture and hide your spelling words within the picture. | Make a shape puzzle for each spelling word. |
|---|---|---|
| f<br>fl<br>fla<br>flag | | big =<br><br>little = |
| Hide each spelling word in a letter path! | Make your own spelling activity. | Write each spelling word and its value.<br><br>Vowel = 2 points<br><br>Consonant = 1 point |
| Write each spelling word two times. | Write each spelling word in a sentence and underline the word. | Rainbow write your words. |

**IEP DRAFT LETTER**

Teacher's Name
School Name
School Street Address
School City, State Zip

Dear Parent,

This is a draft of your child's IEP. The meeting will be held on Date of Meeting at Location of Meeting, according to the meeting notice that you have previously received. The meeting will start at Time of Meeting. Please review this paperwork and write down any questions or comments that you may have. Remember this is only a draft; nothing is set in stone. All items are subject to change to comply with the findings of the IEP Team.

If something prevents you from attending this meeting, please call the school at School Phone Number.

I look forward to meeting with you.


Teacher's Name

**LUNCH AND SPECIALS SCHEDULE**

# Schedule for Lunch & Specials
# Ms. Educator's Kindergarten

Music
Mondays
12:45–1:30 p.m.

Lunch
10:55–11:25 a.m.

P.E.
Tuesday: 10–10:30 a.m.
Wednesday: 12:30–1 p.m.

Guidance
Thursdays
10:00–10:30 a.m.

Library
Thursdays
12:30–1:00 p.m.

Art
Fridays
12:45–1:30 p.m.

**MATH HOMEWORK SAMPLE**

Name _____

Use your math words to complete four activities (one a day).
When you finish an activity, color the box.

| Write your numbers to 30. | Draw a picture using shapes. | Write your numbers by 5's to 30. |
|---|---|---|
| Write your numbers by 10's to 100. | Make your own math activity. | Make a graph of different objects in your home. |
| Make a pattern using shapes or numbers. | Draw a picture of something standing in a line and label each ordinal position. | Write about something you can sort or estimate. Draw a picture to match your sentence. |

**MONTHLY NEWSLETTER SAMPLE**

| ROOM 6 | Your School |
| --- | --- |
| | September Volume 1, Issue 1 |

# Mrs. Teacher's Newsletter

## Welcome

Ms. Assistant and I would like to welcome you to room 6 at Your Elementary School. We are off to a great start. The students are starting to settle into our daily routine as well as the expectations of the room.

In the next few weeks, we will start doing more independent work in a center-type environment. This will give students an opportunity to explore some of the standards of learning on their own, in pairs, or in small groups. This interaction allows students to develop an understanding of the concepts discussed as a whole group by giving them an

opportunity to have discussions with their peers as well as participate in hands-on activities. This also gives the teacher and assistant a chance to work with students in smaller groups or one on one.

In addition, I will start sending home leveled readers this month. PLEASE take a few moments and read with your child and have your child read to you. Look for these readers to come in a gallon-size plastic bag. If readers are not returned or reading tracking sheets are not signed, I will not send out the next set of readers.

## Classroom Job Assignments

Students love to be a part of the learning process. We have several positions that the students can serve in every week. These jobs include being president, vice president, security, secretary, financial officer, or environmental specialist.

## Classroom Expectations

Students are expected to come to class prepared and ready to learn. They should exhibit characteristics that exemplify respect for themselves and for others at all times.

To ensure that these expectations are being upheld, students can earn individual and classroom rewards.

Students have the ability to earn up to "ten" dollars a day, which they can spend in the Room 6 store on Friday.

In addition, students can earn "warm and fuzzies" for exhibiting acts of kindness without being asked. They will also earn "pricklies" when they exhibit behaviors that are hurtful to someone else. If, at the end of the month, they have earned more warm and fuzzies than pricklies, I will purchase a predesignated prize for the students.

For the month of October, the students are working toward pizza.

Consequences include earning less money or losing money for the day, students being excluded from nonacademic rewards given to the class, referrals, calls or notes home, and/or a visit to the principals.

## Mrs. Teacher's Classroom Newsletter  Page 2

## This Month's Assignments

This month we will be working on the following:

**Social Science:** Locating and Interpreting Geographic Information
Physical and Human Characteristics of Ancient Civilizations and locations of Greece, Rome, and West Africa
Contributions of Ancient Greece and Rome
Contributions of the West African Empire of Mali

**Language Arts:**
<u>Explain</u> the author's purpose
Compare the use of fact and fantasy in historical fiction with other forms of literature
Identify major events and supporting details

**Math:**
Number & Number Sense: Whole Numbers
Computation & Estimation: Problem Solving
Number and Number Sense: ( +, - )
Patterns, Functions, & Algebra: Properties

**Science**-Scientific Investigation / Introduction to Science Fair

Matter: Composition & Properties of Matter

Force, Motion, and Energy: Simple Machines
Use Strand Tests: Force, Motion, Energy & Matter, and Scientific Investigation

### Reminders to Students
- Do not forget your homework folder and your agendas.

### Reminders to Parents
- If you have not returned the photo permission forms, please do so as soon as possible.
- If you would like to donate items to the Room 6 store, please send these items in.

## Our Schedule

**Social Science**
8:20–9:10
**Resource**
9:15–9:55
**Language Arts**
10:00–12:00
**Recess**
12:00–12:10
**Lunch**
12:15–12:50
**Math**
12:55–2:10
**Science**
2:15–2:40

*Resource students' schedules may vary.

## Upcoming Events

**Early Dismissal**
Friday, October 8, 20xx
**Parent Teacher Conference Day**
Friday, October 14–15, 20xx
**Interims**
Friday, October 14–15, 20xx
**Fourth Grade field Trip**
Friday, October 29, 20xx

## Contact Information

I can be reached during school hours at (555) 555-5555 or you can email me at <u>teacher@district.us</u>

Ms. Teacher

## OBSERVATION FORM

Student Name: _____ Date: _____

General Education Teacher: _____ Time: _____

Observation Completed By: _____

Observation Notes:

_____

_____

_____

_____

_____

_____

_____

_____

_____

_____

_____

_____

_____

_____

_____

_____

**PROFESSIONAL GOALS AND OBJECTIVES SAMPLE**

**New Teacher**                                          **3–5th Exceptional Education**

October 8, 20xx

**Professional Goals & Objectives**

**I.   Instructional Objectives**
   a.  Objective
       By June 20xx, the students in my class will have completed the statewide assessment that was determined
       by the IEP team with a passing score.

   **Strategies Used to Achieve This Objective**
   - District Pacing Guide
   - District Curriculum Guide
   - Manipulative/ hands-on activities
   - Technology (computer programs, websites, videos, etc.)

   **Evaluation Instruments**
   - Teacher-made Assessments
   - Standards of Learning Assessments
   - VGLA/VAAP books approved by District/State

**II.  Instructional Objectives**
   a.  Objective
       By June 20xx, the students in my class will show an increase in their reading and comprehension levels.

   **Strategies Used to Achieve This Objective**
   - District Pacing Guide
   - Cross Curriculum Learning
   - Manipulative/ hands-on activities
   - Technology (computer programs, websites, videos, etc.)
   - SRA Reading Mastery Program
   - A–Z Reading Activities

   **Evaluation Instruments**
   - Teacher-made Assessments
   - Reading Mastery Assessments
   - A–Z Assessments

**III.   Instructional Objectives**
   a.  Objective
       By June 20xx, I will connect with parents and community leaders to get support for the classroom and the
       school.

   **Strategies Used to Achieve This Objective**
   - Contact local businesses
   - Maintain contact with parents of my students
   - Establish a newsletter

   **Evaluation Instruments**
   - Collection of newsletters
   - List of parent & community volunteers

**READING BOOK BAGS**

Please complete and send back on Thursday with books. New books will **not** be sent out until old books are returned.

|  | Monday | Tuesday | Wednesday | Thursday |
|---|---|---|---|---|
| **Title Read** |  |  |  | Return book to school today |
| **Initial on date read** |  |  |  |  |
| **Notes** <br> **SR—Student Read** <br> **PR—Parent Read** <br> **B—Both** |  |  |  |  |

## BEHAVIOR ROCK LOG

| Name | $10 | $5 | $1 | |
|------|------|------|------|------|
| | ◯ | ◯ | ◯ | |
| | ◯ | ◯ | ◯ | |
| | ◯ | ◯ | ◯ | |
| | ◯ | ◯ | ◯ | |
| | ◯ | ◯ | ◯ | |
| | ◯ | ◯ | ◯ | |
| | ◯ | ◯ | ◯ | |
| | ◯ | ◯ | ◯ | |
| | ◯ | ◯ | ◯ | |
| | ◯ | ◯ | ◯ | |
| | ◯ | ◯ | ◯ | |

## STUDENT BEHAVIOR ROCK LOG

| | | | | |
|---|---|---|---|---|
| Monday | ⬭ | ⬭ | ⬭ | |
| Tuesday | ⬭ | ⬭ | ⬭ | |
| Wednesday | ⬭ | ⬭ | ⬭ | |
| Thursday | ⬭ | ⬭ | ⬭ | |
| Friday | ⬭ | ⬭ | ⬭ | |

## STUDENT BEHAVIOR ROCK LOG

| | | | | |
|---|---|---|---|---|
| Monday | ⬭ | ⬭ | ⬭ | |
| Tuesday | ⬭ | ⬭ | ⬭ | |
| Wednesday | ⬭ | ⬭ | ⬭ | |
| Thursday | ⬭ | ⬭ | ⬭ | |
| Friday | ⬭ | ⬭ | ⬭ | |

**SPELLING CONTRACT**

Name_____ Date_____

**Spelling Words:**                                              Vocabulary:

1.                          6.                          11.
2.                          7.                          12.
3.                          8.                          13.
4.                          9.                          14.
5.                          10.                         15.

**Monday:** Write the words that you missed on the Pretest three times each.

| | | |
|---|---|---|
| 1. | | |
| 2. | | |
| 3. | | |
| 4. | | |
| 5. | | |
| 6. | | |
| 7. | | |
| 8. | | |
| 9. | | |
| 10. | | |
| 11. | | |
| 12. | | |
| 13. | | |
| 14. | | |
| 15. | | |

**Tuesday:** Write the words in Alphabetical Order.

| | | |
|---|---|---|
| 1. | 6. | 11. |
| 2. | 7. | 12. |
| 3. | 8. | 13. |
| 4. | 9. | 14. |
| 5. | 10. | 15. |

**Wednesday:** Pick ten words and use each word in a sentence.

| |
|---|
| 1. |
| 2. |
| 3. |
| 4. |
| 5. |
| 6. |
| 7. |
| 8. |
| 9. |
| 10. |

**Thursday:** Pick two vocabulary words and draw a picture of them.

| | |
|---|---|
| | |

**Remember to study for your Spelling Test!!**

Parent Signature_____

# Appendix F

# Website Listings

These are just some of the websites that the contributors of this book have used over the years. There are many more that you may discover and find useful. Many of these websites are free but some require membership fees.

** Websites that cover more than one subject.

### Language Arts
http://www.starfall.com

http://www.vrml.k12.la.us/sadies/links/reading/reading_links.htm

http://www.pbs.org/teachers

http://www2.scholastic.com

http://www.arcademicskillbuilders.com

http://www.funbrain.com

http://www.spellingcity.com

http://www.readinga-z.com

http://www.eduplace.com

http://www.readwritethink.org

http://www.brainpop.com**

http://www.brainpopjr.com**

http://www.literactive.com

http://www.reading.org

http://www.tumblebooks.com

http://streaming.discoveryeducation.com**

### Mathematics
http://www.fun4thebrain.com**

http://www.bbc.co.uk/schools/ks2bitesize/maths/data/interpreting_data/play.shtml

http://illuminations.nctm.org

http://www.enchantedlearning.com**

http://www.aaamath.com

http://www.aplusmath.com

http://www.gamequarium.com/math.htm

http://www.funbrain.com/brain/MathBrain/MathBrain.html

http://quizhub.com/quiz/quizhub.cfm**

### Science/ Social Studies
http://sv.berkeley.edu/showcase/flash/fish.html

http://www.activescience-gsk.com/module2/home.html

http://www.sciencea-z.com

http://edsitement.neh.gov

http://www.bbc.co.uk/schools/ks2bitesize/index.shtml**

http://www.ipl.org/div/kidspace**

http://www.smithsonianeducation.org/students

http://www.nwf.org/Kids/Ranger-Rick.aspx

http://kids.nationalgeographic.com/kids

http://www.billnye.com

http://www.epa.gov/kids

http://www.nasa.gov/audience/forkids/kidsclub/flash/index.html

http://www.weeklyreader.com**

### Professional/Teacher Associations
http://www.ascd.org (formally the Association for Supervision and Curriculum Development)

http://www.nsta.org (National Science Teacher Association)

http://www.nctm.org (National Council of Teachers of Mathematics)

http://www.socialstudies.org (National Council for the Social Studies)

http://www.ncte.org (National Council of Teachers of English)

http://www.ceai.org (Christian Educators Association International)

http://www.naset.org (National Association of Special Education Teachers)

http://www.nea.org (National Education Association)

http://www.aft.org (American Federation of Teachers)

http://www.naeyc.org (National Association for the Education of Young Children)

http://www.nbpts.org (National Board for Professional Teaching Standards)

http://www.ncpie.org (National Coalition for Parent Involvement in Education)

http://www.nhsa.net (National Head Start Association)

http://www.nmsa.org (National Middle School Association)

http://www.pta.org (National Parent Teacher Association)

http://www.pdkintl.org (Phi Delta Kappa Professional Education Association)

**Miscellaneous**

http://www.education.com**

http://www.discoveryeducation.com**

http://www.scholastic.com/kids/homework

http://www.timesaversforteachers.com

http://www.adoptaclassroom.org

http://www.ed.gov

http://www.coollessons.org

http://www.internet4classrooms.com

http://www.superteacherworksheets.com

**Students with Disabilities**

http://www.cec.sped.org (Council for Exceptional Children)

http://www.educationoasis.com

http://www.ttaconline.org

http://www.chadd.org (Children and Adults with Attention Deficit/Hyperactivity Disorder)

http://www.learningally.org

http://www.ldpride.net

http://www.rti4success.org

# References

Ackerman, Becky. 2007. *P.R.A.I.S.E.: Effectively Guiding Student Behavior.* Colorado Springs, CO: Purposeful Design Publications.

Bryer, Jeanna. 2005. "Rewards Not Working?" *Instructor* 115 (4): 19–20, 52.

Gillespie, Marilyn K. 2002. *EFF Research Principle: A Purposeful and Transparent Approach to Teaching and Learning.* Washington, DC: National Institute for Literacy.

IES National Center for Education Evaluation and Regional Assistance. 2009. *Comprehensive Teacher Induction.* July. Washington, DC: NCEE Evaluation Brief.

Jones, Fred. 2007. *Tools for Teaching: Discipline, Instruction, Motivation.* 2nd ed. Santa Cruz, CA: Fredric H. Jones & Associates, Inc.

Kelly, Melissa. 2008. *180 Tips and Tricks for New Teachers.* Avon, MA: Adams Media.

Krajnjan, Stevan. 2009. *Timesavers for Teachers.* San Francisco, CA: Jossey-Bass.

Miller, Debbie. 2008. *Teaching with Intention: Defining Beliefs, Aligning Practice, Taking Action K–5.* Portland, ME: Stenhouse Publishers.

Thompson, Julia G. 2007. *The First-Year Teacher's Survival Guide.* San Francisco, CA: Jossey-Bass.

———. 2009. *The First-Year Teacher's Checklist.* San Francisco, CA: Jossey-Bass.